THE MEANING OF EPHESIANS

THE MEANING OF EPHESIANS

By
EDGAR J. GOODSPEED

WIPF & STOCK · Eugene, Oregon

Wipf and Stock Publishers
199 W 8th Ave, Suite 3
Eugene, OR 97401

The Meaning of Ephesians
By Goodspeed, Edgar J.
ISBN 13: 978-1-62032-078-5
Publication date 3/15/2012
Previously published by University of Chicago Press, 1933

TO CLAYTON R. BOWEN
STIMULATING SCHOLAR AND
GENEROUS FRIEND

PREFACE

Among the books of the New Testament, none is more in need of clarification than the Letter to the Ephesians. The traditional view of its origin has clearly broken down, as the efforts of those who hold it to interpret the letter abundantly show. On the other hand the historical approach has not succeeded in establishing a probable origin for it which can stand in the presence of the well-known facts of criticism and find a convincing meaning in every part of the letter. Yet these critical facts should lead us unerringly to the origin of the letter, and the origin, if rightly determined, should in turn unfold the meaning of the letter.

It is the endeavor of this book to follow these facts as clues toward the solution of an unsolved problem of New Testament study; to formulate the conclusion to which they lead; and to review the thought of the letter in the light of this conclusion, on the principle that if the conclusion is sound, the letter should take on new meaning and force, and respond more luminously to the process of interpretation than it has done hitherto—in short, to solve the riddle of Ephesians.

The positions developed here have already been sketched briefly in *The Formation of the New Testament* (1926), and more fully in *New Solutions of New Testament Problems* (1927). They were widely challenged with a demand for supporting evidence. This very proper demand I have undertaken to meet in these pages with evidence of two kinds: first, the interpretation of Ephesians, which proves to be much more luminous and significant when approached in this way; and, second, the detailed exhibit of Pauline parallels to Ephesians, which is inexplicable on any other theory of the origin of the epistle.

My friends, Mr. James R. Branton and Mr. Alfred E. Haefner, have helped me with the reading of the proof, and I am much indebted to many students and friends for criticism, suggestion, and encouragement. I may mention my colleagues, Dr. Donald W. Riddle, Dr. Harold R. Willoughby, and Dr. Ernest C. Colwell, and particularly my learned friend and neighbor, Professor Clayton R. Bowen.

EDGAR J. GOODSPEED

November 1, 1932

PART I
THE OCCASION AND MEANING OF EPHESIANS

Eine klare Vorstellung ueber die Situation, in der ein Paulus redivivus den Eph. verfasst hat, is bisher nicht beschaffen worden.—JUELICHER, *Einleitung in das Neue Testament* (5th ed.), p. 127.

INTRODUCTION

Ephesians is a great rhapsody on the worth of the Christian salvation. Like Hebrews, it belongs to an age when men had had time to reflect on the value of the new faith to mankind. It is cast not in argumentative but in meditative, almost liturgical, forms; it breathes a spirit of reflection and adoration. This liturgical power reminds us of the Revelation. Thus its mood and its method alike have their closest parallels in the last decade of the first century.

In form it is an encyclical, for its first sentence addresses Christians everywhere. This again is the spirit of the tenth decade, when, as in I Peter, the Christians of five provinces might be addressed in a letter. This is as great a contrast to primitive attitudes and situations as are its liturgical power and interest. In the tenth decade the church began to show that genius for liturgy which Walter Pater called one of her great endowments.

The situation is twofold. Schism is threatening the churches; the sects are beginning to appear. Our first hint of this development is in Luke-Acts, a work written not far from A.D.90.[1] In the two generations that followed, heretical movements honeycombed the church. The time demanded a stirring call to unity among the churches. This Ephesians nobly supplied.

And the Pauline letters have been discovered. This is the second element in the situation. They had been written in the heat and toil of the Greek mission, and fallen into obscurity, as most old letters do. The ignorance of the early

[1] See Goodspeed, *New Solutions of New Testament Problems*, pp. 94–103.

evangelists of them—Mark, Matthew, Luke—shows this unmistakably. And besides, their enduring worth would not be at once apparent, for they must have seemed to their recipients wholly concerned with immediate local problems and situations. The silence of Mark, Matthew, and Luke-Acts about them is therefore entirely natural. In their days the Pauline letters had not been collected and published.

What could have terminated this neglect and led to their collection and circulation? Probably the publication of Luke-Acts, with its striking account of Paul's work in the Greek mission and its inimitable sketch of Paul himself. That work must have recalled Christian attention to Paul and with its account of the churches he had founded may well have led to a search among them for other letters of his than the one or two known to the searcher. The fact that the collected letters are first reflected in the literature immediately following Luke-Acts lends color to this hypothesis. They were unknown to the author of Luke-Acts, but directly after they are well known.

But how came the collectors of the letters to know that any existed at all, and ever to think of the possibility of a collection? They must have had direct knowledge that Paul wrote at least some letters to the churches; in all probability there existed in their own church a letter of his, which was kept alive in a sense, probably by being read in church on the anniversary of his martyrdom.[2]

---

[2] The easy assumption of some writers on introduction and canon that Paul's letters must have been regularly read in public worship from the time of their composition is definitely negatived by the testimony of Justin, who shows that in Ephesus and Rome the gospels were read in church in the second quarter of the second century, but not the letters of Paul (*Apology* 67:3).

Colossians is the letter of Paul's most familiar to the writer of Ephesians, and this encourages the impression that it was the nucleus of the Pauline collection; the letter which upon the appearance of Luke-Acts suggested to its possessors that the Pauline churches mentioned in that work might also have preserved letters of his, and that a collection of these, after the pattern of the collected letters of Plato, or of Epicurus, might be of value. Acts would have guided the collectors to Galatia, Philippi, Thessalonica, Ephesus, Corinth, and Rome, as churches with Pauline associations, where letters might reasonably be sought. But Acts would never have guided a Roman or a Corinthian collector to Colossae, for it does not mention that place.

Imagine a man already possessed of one letter of Paul's, which he had found in occasional use in a local church in Asia, finding in the Acts the story of its writer and his work in the founding or development of half-a-dozen churches. He has never known so much of the career of the apostle before, and the thought strikes him, What if there are other letters of his still existing among these Pauline churches? A few years later Polycarp of Smyrna, a man of the Ephesian circle, made such a collection of the letters of Ignatius, and sent them about among churches that asked for them, like that at Philippi. And the Acts with its stirring account of the missionary work of Paul might well move a man who had one Pauline letter to look or inquire at Philippi, Thessalonica, Corinth, and other places where Acts said he had labored, for possible remaining letters of his.

This is not all imagination. The writer of Ephesians had clearly known Colossians longer than the other letters of

Paul, yet he had come to know them all. He also knew Luke-Acts, with its story of Paul's work among the Greeks.[3] There is no evidence of the circulation of Paul's letters before the publication of Luke-Acts, but the writer of Ephesians knows them all, and from that time on they continue to be well known. Luke-Acts would naturally interest him afresh in Paul, and the possession of one or two letters of his would naturally lead him to think that others might be found in the Pauline churches of which Acts informed him. The collection arose from the effect upon a man possessed of Colossians-Philemon, of the story of Paul's work in the Greek cities recorded in the Acts. These facts cannot be related in any more natural sequence. They point unmistakably to the conclusion that the writer of Ephesians was also the collector of the Pauline letters.

If Colossians was the germ of the collection, as these two facts suggest, it almost certainly already had with it Philemon, which is doubtless that long-sought letter from Laodicea mentioned in Col. 4:16. For (1) Paul's remark in that passage would bring the two letters together, in the chests of both churches; (2) Philemon is really a church letter, for it is addressed to the church that meets in Philemon's house; (3) Archippus is mentioned in Col. 4:17 as though he were not a Colossian ("Tell Archippus," not "and do you, Archippus") but a Laodicean: "Have the letter read in the church at Laodicea, ... and tell Archippus." The sense is all too plain: Archippus, who is probably the minister of the church in Philemon's house—"our fellow-soldier Archippus"—has the trying duty of seeing that Philemon receives the wayward Onesimus humanely,

[3] For evidence of these two positions see Part II of this work.

instead of punishing him with all the cruelty which Roman law ordained.[4] The Christian sentiment of the churches of Colossae and Laodicea is brought to bear upon Philemon, to insure the safety of the runaway Onesimus. (4) This explains the presence of "Philemon" in what was obviously a collection of Paul's letters to churches; it was as a church letter that it must have gained admittance to the collection. Moreover (5) the spurious Laodiceans, extant in Latin in about one hundred manuscripts, is just the length of our Philemon, as though it were written to fit a traditional measure recorded in some ancient stichometrical list, for the original Laodiceans.

On the other hand, if Philemon is not "the letter from Laodicea," how did it get into the collection of church letters? Its presence becomes a problem. And what has become of "the letter from Laodicea" which Paul's words in Col. 3:16 lead us to expect to find from the earliest times associated with Colossians, in the chests of both churches?

A collector of Paul's letters to churches would not be likely to include Philemon. But if it was already part of the original nucleus of the Pauline collection, as "the letter from Laodicea," it could hardly be displaced. The problem of Philemon is on any other view a difficult one. But if it

[4] Slavery is so disagreeable a subject that it has been almost obliterated from the English New Testament. As a matter of fact, however, Philemon might have gone to any length in punishing Onesimus, as a slave who had robbed him and run away. Thievish and runaway slaves were branded on the forehead. The testimony of slaves was regularly taken by torture. The Lex Petrocia (probably under Augustus) forbade a master to compel his slave to fight with wild beasts—unless the authorities decided that the slave deserved it! Juvenal (*Satire* vi) speaks of the crucifying of slaves for slight faults and realistically describes the brutal whipping of them. In the fifth mime of Herodas, a woman sends her slave off to be whipped to death though she later relents. It was a very serious thing to send Onesimus back into the power of his master, and Paul must have taken every possible measure to protect him from harm.

was "the letter from Laodicea," all these difficulties disappear.[5]

We may therefore think of Colossians and Philemon (=Laodiceans) as constituting the nucleus of the Pauline collection; and even of Paul himself as having, quite unconsciously, given in Col. 4:16 the first impulse toward it.

But Ephesians is no mere second edition of Colossians, greatly as it is indebted to it. It is true that three-fifths of Colossians is reflected in Ephesians. But so are all the other Pauline letters known to us. It shows abundant use of Romans, I Corinthians, II Corinthians, Philippians, and Galatians, and limited but unmistakable use of I Thessalonians, II Thessalonians, and Philemon. Ephesians is a mosaic of Pauline materials; it is almost a Pauline anthology; it is altogether built of Pauline elements, even though the writer goes well beyond Paul in the use he makes of them. Indeed, it may be doubted whether Paul himself was ever in such a position to survey and summarize his own thought and message as the author of Ephesians was. It has been

---

[5] The ἐξ ὑμῶν of Col. 4:9 is generally urged as evidence that Onesimus and hence Philemon lived in Colossae. But it must be remembered that Laodicea and Colossae were so close together as to be almost contiguous, being some ten miles apart on the road that ran through the Lycus glen in Phrygia. Paul cannot mean that Onesimus is a member of the Colossian church; ὑμῶν is certainly used in a wider sense than that. In how wide a sense then? It is artificial to extend it to the city and refuse to extend it to the region of the Lycus Valley, including Laodicea. That Paul sometimes thinks of the Colossians and Laodiceans together in writing Colossians is suggested by 2:1: "for you and for our brothers in Laodicea, and for all who do not know me personally." The passage 4:9 cannot be taken as proving that Onesimus was a Colossian; it is quite satisfied by the fact that he came from that part of the Lycus Valley.

But even if 4:9 did establish the Colossian *origin* of Onesimus (cf. Rom. 9:5, ἐξ ὧν ὁ Χριστός), it would not make Philemon a Colossian, for Archippus is definitely a third person to the Colossians and Paul (4:17); he is a townsman of Philemon (Philemon, vs. 2) and is introduced in Colossians in a connection that points unmistakably to Laodicea. There is no escaping this; Archippus is not a Colossian, and the implication of 4:15-17 is that he was a Laodicean.

well said that Ephesians reads like a commentary on the Pauline letters.

Almost every line of Ephesians shows the literary influence of the known letters of Paul. What is more astonishing and significant, however—these letters almost completely satisfy his materials; that is, he seems to have used them and practically nothing else, except some touches from Luke-Acts and the Septuagint.

Out of 618 short phrases into which Ephesians may be conveniently broken for detailed comparison with the Pauline letters, 550 have unmistakable parallels in Paul, in words or substance. These parallels are with every part of Ephesians, and they are found in all the nine genuine letters of Paul. They constitute a major feature of the Ephesian problem, which cannot be soundly treated without full consideration of them. They are fatal to the traditional assignment of the letter to Paul, and they put the current critical theory of a Paulinist author writing in the eighties, before the Pauline letters were collected, completely out of court. That position is a demonstrable impossibility. The problem of Ephesians is inextricably intertwined with that of the Pauline corpus; it cannot be dealt with apart from it. I hope that those who think differently or have any doubt about this will take the pains to work through the survey of Ephesians and its Pauline parallels in the second part of this volume.

Paul himself could hardly have so rigidly confined himself to what he had previously written, still less to just that part of what he had written which has come down to us. He certainly had more ideas than happen to be preserved in our nine letters, and in every one of his genuine letters he unfolds some new area of thought and expression. The writer of Ephesians has no such command of the mind of Paul; he knows it only through a careful and thorough study of the nine genuine letters, which made up the first collection.

The writer of Ephesians was thus the earliest student of the letters of Paul—indeed, we may truly say, the first interpreter of them. His own letter, which may fairly be called an epistle, is in a sense a commentary upon them. This is the evident meaning of the facts just described.

The world is still concerned with the religious values of the Pauline letters, and the impression they must have produced upon the first beholder of them can be faintly imagined. It overwhelmed him with all the force of a revelation. No one of the churches to which they were addressed had ever seen them assembled in all their variety and vigor, and the first collector of them must have felt like the discoverer of a new world of religious values and techniques. He was himself of course already a Christian, but how meager his Christianity must have appeared in comparison with that of the great religious genius whose experience and inner life now stood revealed before him, as it had been to no man before! If such an experience would not explain a rhapsody upon the Christian salvation, it is difficult to see what would. To cast the Pauline gospel into this great inspired reflection, this great liturgical meditation upon the supreme worth of Christianity was a natural result of such an experience, on the part of the extraordinary man who wrote Ephesians.

It is as though the letters of Paul had been gathering, dammed up behind the obstacle of their private-letter style, until Ephesians breaks a way through for them, and forms the cascade by which their refreshing waters reach the churches. To adopt the alternative that they leaked gradually and obscurely into circulation is not only at variance with all the literary evidence (the silence of Mark, Matthew, and Luke), but leaves the origin of Ephesians inexplicable.

Of course this great treasure of Christian understanding must be given to the churches, and what more necessary and appropriate than to preface it with the collector's own impression of the values it enshrined? The need of the second generation of Christianity was to be reassured of the worth of the faith it had inherited; Hebrews is the unquestioned illustration of this, and the Revelation complains that the church at Ephesus has "left its first love." To the same age belongs also Ephesians, which essays the same task, but in a different way; less argumentatively and allegorically; more confidently and intuitively.

Of all these interests, then, Ephesians is the resultant. It commends the collected Pauline letters to the churches, which are really one and so entitled to read and profit by them all. The seven-fold character of the collection, the *typus septiformis ecclesiae*, happily symbolized this to the ancient mind. As the Muratorian writer a century later said of John, Paul in writing to seven churches wrote to all. This is the point of the account of Paul in chapter 3, which Burton considered a transition and Moule a digression. It is from one point of view the high point of the epistle, which here commends Paul, as the bearer of this gospel, to his readers. The letters of Paul were very obviously specific in occasion and destination. Ephesians generalized their message in the mood of its own day, and directed all Christians to find in them a further account of that amazing mystery of which he had been an interpreter.

This opens the way for that call to unity among the churches which the rising sects so seriously menaced. They must remember that they are one. This is the real meaning of the death of Christ. Old barriers are down; Jew and Greek are no more. Under this old form, the writer puts forward his appeal for unity among the Greek churches in the face of the rising sects. And what can do more to unite these churches than this collection of the letters of their great founder? They can now find in them inspiration and instruction that will safeguard them against the schismatics and unite them in Christian truth.

A Scottish minister recently contributed to the *Atlantic Monthly* "The Epistle of Kallikrates," supposedly written by a Corinthian Christian in reply to I Corinthians, and newly discovered.[6] Why did he adopt this quaint method of discussing the practical problems of modern religious life? Because it would attract attention and gain him a hearing. Has anyone reproached him for it? I do not think so. So modern a thing is pseudepigraphy. The writer of Ephesians boldly ascribed his epistle to Paul, from whom he had in fact taken almost every line of it; and he is called a pseudepigrapher. If he had put his own name at the head of it, the same people would have called him a plagiarist. It is clear that we cannot deal with ancient literature, nor indeed with modern, in this short and easy fashion. Is the Philocalia by Origen, or is it not? Yes or No?

To these early Christians in fact writing was a social

[6] *Atlantic Monthly*, March, 1928.

process. They did not seek to advertise themselves. They preferred to disappear behind the books they helped to put in form. The earliest gospels were anonymous. The writer of Ephesians was well aware that he was in no full sense the author of his epistle. Seeking nothing for himself, he sought to honor Paul and serve his generation as best he could. We would doubtless have done it differently, but possibly not so well.

But it is surely very artificial to deny pseudepigraphy to an age that could freely compose the Pauline and other speeches in the Acts and actually put forth the Revelation of John as written at the dictation of Jesus himself. A few years later the Roman church took the great name of Peter in addressing the churches of Asia Minor on a grave matter of Christian attitude. But it is not our task here to establish the non-Pauline character of Ephesians. That has been done by others, long since. That Ephesians is an encyclical is also the clear verdict of the textual evidence. It is our present purpose rather to accept these clear facts of literary study, and to proceed to build upon them, convinced that we shall thus learn more about the extraordinary story of early Christianity than we shall by forever trying to explain them away.

This is abundantly clear from the experience of those scholars who have chosen the latter path and persist in ascribing Ephesians to Paul. They find themselves with the letter on their hands to be fitted into the life and thought of Paul, and into the situations of his time. This task is too much for even the ablest and most competent of them, and no wonder, for it is an impossible one. "The apostle himself," says Burton,[7] "almost disappears from view." "Paul wrote it, if one might say so," says Professor Scott, "for his own satisfaction.". . . . "Ephesians, more than anything else he wrote, is a private meditation, but he composed it as an epistle, for the benefit of a particular group of readers. . . . . We know nothing of the church he wrote to, not even its name. In any case his purpose must have been a quite general one, for he had never visited this community, and cannot have known much of its special difficulties."[8] Is it not plain that, having convinced themselves that the letter is by Paul, these scholars do not know what to do with it? It refuses to fit into his career or method. They see in it only an arrow shot vaguely into the air, chiefly for the satisfaction of the archer.

It is the glory of historical interpretation that when once the situation that called forth a document is determined, the document at once becomes luminous with meaning. The penalty of it is, that if that situation is not soundly determined, the document remains lost in obscurity. It does not yield its meaning. Judged by this matter-of-fact test, the effort to understand Ephesians in the life of Paul must be adjudged a failure, for it does not illumine the epistle; it obscures it. The apostle seems to be talking *to* himself, but not talking *like* himself. No particular situation emerges. No particular church or churches seem to be addressed. Contrast this with a situation like that of I Corinthians, where we know so definitely to whom he is writing and what he is writing about; or of Galatians, written to a whole group of churches.

[7] *Handbook of the Life of Paul*, p. 88. [8] *Colossians, Philemon, Ephesians*, p. 123.

The main tenor of the epistle seems on this theory to be unexplained: the great jubilation over the worth of the Christian religion. This is so out of place in the ministry of Paul that most of the Pauline interpreters actually miss it altogether. Nothing could more completely establish the failure of the Pauline approach to get the meaning out of the epistle, or exhibit more convincingly the bankruptcy of the traditional exegesis.

Ephesians is the Waterloo of commentators. It baffles them. This is mainly because they have not found out the situation that called it forth. We have seen that it cannot be fitted successfully into Paul's life or thought; and Juelicher long ago remarked that no "clear hypothesis of the circumstances under which a *Paulus redivivus* might have composed the Epistle to the Ephesians has ever been provided. . . . ."

It is the purpose of these pages to propose such a hypothesis as Juelicher desiderated, and to show how admirably the epistle fits into the situation that is proposed for it.

It is the second generation of Greek Christianity. Men and women who have come by their religion by inheritance need to be reminded of its extraordinary worth. This need is reflected also in the Revelation and in Hebrews.

The sects are beginning to appear, and are undermining the unity of the churches. This is a situation glimpsed in the Acts, and definitely reflected in the Revelation. The churches must be warned against them. There is a Church Universal, to which believers belong.

The letters of Paul have been found, and collected, and are about to be published. Since our earliest reflections of them, apart from Ephesians, reflect Ephesians along with them, it seems clear that Ephesians appeared as part of the collection from its first publication.[9] But what place can such an encyclical, bridging the gap between Paul's day and its own, have had in such a collection, except to begin and introduce it, just as the first chapter of the Revelation introduces the messages to the seven churches, with a general letter to all seven? In this we may see the earliest reflection of the original Pauline corpus: the prophet of Ephesus was so impressed by it that he actually began his apocalypse with a corpus of letters to seven churches.[10]

To set forth the transcendent value of the Christian faith for a generation of Greek Christians in danger of forgetting it, to rally the scattered churches to a sense of their essential solidarity, to bridge the gap between Paul's day and his own with a summary of the new-found Pauline teaching in terms of the writer's own day, and to commend the assembled letters of Paul to Christians everywhere—these are the elements which this great unknown soon after the publication of the Acts combined into a letter so good that many people still insist that it must be the work of Paul himself. But its exalted and sustained liturgical style is unlike Paul, and altogether in line with the trend of the Revelation, Hebrews, and the Lucan canticles.

The religio-historical approach leads us by firm and clear steps to this view of the epistle, and the literary considerations, both specific and general, strongly confirm it. The special non-Pauline element in the vocabulary, for example,

---

[9] Lightfoot observes that Clement of Rome "shows that he is imbued with the Epistles to the Romans, Corinthians and Ephesians" (*Clement of Rome*, I, 397), and recognizes the use of Eph. 4:4 f. in I Clem. 46:6 (II, 140).

[10] The contents and early history of the first collection of Paul's letters I have undertaken to outline in *New Solutions of New Testament Problems*, chap. v.

fits surprisingly well in a work written after Luke-Acts and before the Revelation, Hebrews, and I Peter.[11]

But the most searching test for this or any other theory as to the origin of the epistle is how the interpretation responds to it. Does the proposed account of the origin of the epistle, as a summary of Pauline Christianity, an affirmation of its worth, a demand for Christian unity in the face of the sects, and a commendation of the collected Pauline letters to Christians everywhere, make it any more luminous and significant? Let us see.

[11] The words used in Ephesians and elsewhere in the New Testament but not in the accepted Pauline letters curiously confirm the suggestion that Ephesians belongs in the period of Acts-Revelation-Hebrews-I Peter. The words men used at a given time are on the whole some index of what people were thinking about at that time.

Acts	ἄγνοια I Pet.	Lk. Acts	πατριά
Mk. Lk.	ἀγρυπνεῖν Heb.	Lk.	περιζωννύναι Rev.
	ἀκρογωνιαῖος I Pet.		πλάτος Rev.
Mt. Lk. Acts	ἀμφότεροι	Mk. Mt. Lk.	ποιμήν Heb. I Pet. John
Mk. Mt. Lk. Acts	ἄνεμος Rev. John, Jas., Ju.	Acts	πολιτεία
		Mt. Lk.	σαπρός
Acts	ἀνιέναι Heb.		σπίλος II Pet.
Mk. Mt. Lk. Acts	ἅπας John, Jas., I Tim.	Lk.	συνκαθίζειν
Acts	ἀπειλή	Lk. Acts	σωτήριον
Mt. Lk. Acts	διάβολος Rev. Heb. I Pet. John Jas Ju.	Mk. Mt. Lk. Acts	ὕδωρ Rev. Heb. I, II Pet. I John Jas.
	εὔσπλαγχνος I Pet.	Mk. Acts	ὑποδεῖσθαι
Mk. Mt. Lk. Acts	μακράν John	Lk.	ὕψος Rev. Jas.
Mk. Mt. Lk.	ὀργίζεσθαι Rev.	Mk. Mt. Lk.	φραγμός
Lk.	ὅσιοτης	Lk.	φρόνησις
Mk. Mt. Lk. Acts	ὀσφῦς Heb. I Pet.	Lk.	χαριτοῦν
Lk.	πανοπλία	Mk. Acts	χειροποίητος Heb.
Acts	πάροικος I Pet.		

I
1:1, 2

Salutation

Paul, by God's will an apostle of Christ Jesus, to God's people who are steadfast in Christ Jesus; God our Father and the Lord Jesus Christ bless you and give you peace.

The salutation "Paul, by God's will an apostle of Christ Jesus" reproduces precisely the language of II Corinthians. But here, as elsewhere only in Romans among the genuine letters, Paul appears alone, with no colleague in the authorship of the letter. "To God's people who are steadfast in Christ Jesus" is modeled upon Col. 1:2, but here the encyclical address, read by the two most ancient manuscripts, and supported by Origen and Basil, speaks to all Greek Christians, as Paul himself would hardly have thought of doing. For in the generation since his death Paul has grown to hero-stature, as the account of him in the Acts clearly shows. Its record of his relation to Greek Christianity is enough to justify representing him as speaking to Greek Christians everywhere; and his appended letters establish his status as a writer of letters to churches. Having written to them all (the seven-fold church) severally, he may now address them as one. Perhaps the limited encyclical of the Jerusalem apostles in Acts, chapter 15, may have suggested this form to the writer. Certainly in the presence of (1) the Acts and (2) the collected letters, it becomes entirely natural.

To give Paul's name to a summary of his gospel and his morals, almost every line of which is taken from Paul, is really not so very different from giving it to those shortened forms of his letters published a few years ago in *The Shorter New Testament*. The genuine letters, it must be remembered, with the possible exception of Romans, were absorbed with immediate local situations, in themselves of no general interest to other churches. Their lasting religious values would not be at once apparent to the following generation, which might easily dismiss them as just a mass of old letters addressed to other people and concerned with men and matters now dead and gone. To get people to look (as the whole world is now trained to do) past these externals to the enduring inner values of the letters—this was the aim of Ephesians. That we today can hardly persuade ourselves that such a thing ever needed to be done only shows how well the writer of Ephesians did it.

II
1:3–14

Blessed be the God and Father of our Lord Jesus Christ, who through Christ has blessed us with every spiritual blessing in the heavenly realm. Through him he chose us out before the creation of the world, to be consecrated and above reproach in his sight in love. He foreordained us to become his sons through Jesus Christ, in fulfilment of his generous purpose, so that we might praise the splendid blessing which he has given us through his beloved Son. It is through union with him and through his blood that we have been delivered and our offenses forgiven, in the abundance of his mercy which he has lavished upon us. He has given us perfect insight into his secret purpose and understanding of it, in following out the design he planned to carry out in Christ, and in arranging, when the time should have fully come, that everything in heaven and on earth should be unified in Christ—the Christ through whom it is our lot to have been predestined by the design of him who in everything carries out the purpose of his will, to win praise for his glory, by having been the first to believe in Christ. You also have heard the message of the truth, the good news of your salvation, and believed in him, and through union with him you have been marked with the seal of the holy Spirit that was promised, which is the advance instalment of our inheritance, so that we may get full possession of it, and praise his glory for it.

Jubilant Summary of Pauline Doctrine

The first and second chapters constitute a summary of Pauline Christianity, in the form of a *Jubilate* over the blessedness of the Christian salvation. The value of this magnificent Pauline liturgy to the early church, so long dependent upon Jewish patterns in worship, must have been immense. It constitutes a glorious prelude to the Pauline letters. It is like the overture of an opera, foreshadowing the successive melodies that are to follow. All these great aspects of Christian truth and experience the reader was to find more fully dealt with in the letters themselves, of which this was simply a foretaste. The materials of which it is composed are drawn from the letters, but the form, an exalted meditation, in a triumphant, rhapsodical strain, is the writer's own creation.

The special appropriateness of this declaration of the worth of Christianity in the tenth decade is shown by the efforts of the Revelation and Hebrews to supply it. Second-generation Greek Christianity needed to be reminded of the religious values it had inherited, and Ephesians does this in those lofty liturgical forms of which primitive Christian worship stood in need. Ephesians marks the beginning of a new day of nobler forms of worship.[1] This liturgical effect is in part secured, as my colleague Dr. Ernest C. Colwell points out, by its substantive style; the number of nouns per page is markedly greater than in the letters of Paul.

With swift, sure strokes the writer passes in review the leading Pauline ideas (1:3–14). It is difficult to see why anyone should have done this except to bring Paul and his teaching strongly and attractively before his public, which

[1] This is my own personal impression, and I am glad to find it admirably expressed long ago, by Holtzmann:

The author "is especially familiar with the liturgical language which at this time was taking shape; it is the rhetoric of the cultus which gives to his style the fullness and pleonasm of expression which have often been noted, a certain tautological solemnity. The author lives in a time which has already begun to accustom itself to liturgical rhetoric and to feel the need of it. Out of the sonorous ring of certain words and phrases similar effects are produced on these (readers, hearers) as later came forth from church music. Indeed, our letter makes contact with the history of hymnology." "Es ist eine feine und richtige Bemerkung Ewalds, wenn er in dem dichterischen Schwung der Sprache, in der 'Kunst ihrer springenden Saetze,' aber nicht minder auch in einzelnen Lieblingsausdruecken wie τὰ ἐπουράνια, Abhaengigkeit von Lauten des aeltesten Gemeindegesangs erkennt" (Holtzmann, pp. 313, 314).

he must of course have felt greatly needed the vital vigor of the Pauline faith.

How blessed is the Christian lot! Chosen for consecration, foreordained to sonship, forgiven, enlightened, evangelized, and endowed with the spirit: The paragraph strikes the keynote of the epistle. Bacon says of this passage, "Eph. 1:3-14 is constructed on the rhythmic plan of one of those 'spiritual songs and hymns' of Redemption which are referred to in Eph. 5:19," one of which "has actually been quoted in 5:14." He elsewhere describes it as a "long and rhapsodical Thanksgiving," the "exalted lyric of the Thanksgiving."[2] This sublime reflection, polished and generalized, upon the leading features of Pauline religion is one of the first manifestations of the early Christian genius for liturgy. The devotion of the mystery cults to litanies and liturgies must have contributed to this movement, which was destined so greatly to enrich Christian worship.

The thanksgiving opens with a line from II Corinthians: "Blessed be the God and Father of our Lord Jesus Christ!" where it stands in the same position as here. But there it is the expression of Paul's personal sense of comfort and relief; here it serves to introduce the summary of the chief elements in the Christian's blessedness. Every line, as will be shown elsewhere, is drawn from the letters of Paul, but no single idea is dwelt upon or developed; all are swiftly surveyed and passed in review. II Corinthians, Galatians, I Corinthians, Philippians, Romans, Colossians, II Thessalonians, are drawn upon in rapid succession, in no slavish fashion, but by one who has clearly made himself master

[2] *Harvard Theological Review*, 1915, pp. 511, 520.

of their materials. These, as Holtzmann pointed out, he sometimes colors with the liturgical expressions current in his day; there is a curious reverberating quality about the style of Ephesians that can be explained in no other way.

Now and then a line or two of Ephesians seems to summarize a long passage in Paul. Verse 6 seems to sum up a whole paragraph in Romans (5:1-11). "That everything in heaven and on earth should be unified in Christ" (vs. 10*b*) is not, for the writer of Ephesians, simply a gratifying theological reflection, but bears importantly upon the matter of the unity of the churches, so imperiled in his day.

The writer classes himself (as Paul) with those first believers whose salvation was a special source of glory to God. To believe the gospel now, after it has become triumphant, is one thing; it was a greater thing to see its worth when it was new and still obscure. This glorification of the first generation of believers is in itself a significant index of date. In verses 13 and 14, "You also have heard the message of the truth," the readers are contrasted with the first generation of Christians who were "the first to hear."[3]

The enthusiastic summary of Pauline thought may be compared with the prologue of the Gospel of John, in its relation to what followed it. The principal Pauline doctrines are rapidly sketched, with no supporting argument, but as though already established and needing only to be touched upon.

While this overture is in form bold and free, it is at the same time built to an amazing degree out of recognizable Pauline materials, drawn from the extant letters. And this is not strange if its purpose was to offer in inspiring form

[3] Cf. Heb. 2:3.

the heart of the Pauline message, the leading ideas of his letters stripped of the occasional and personal, and presented in their larger general aspect. This may well explain why it should seem, as Robinson says of it, to "baffle any analysis." It is a review of great Pauline ideas, one after another, so rapid that they seem to tumble over one another in their tumultuous course.

The writer does not need to support or develop these great positions; that is all done in the Pauline letters that follow. It is perfectly plain that he is not here working out these ideas; he is supplied with them by the Pauline letters, and has only to sketch them in rapid outline, in all their prodigality of religious power. This rapid survey forms an effective preface for his great appeal to his readers (1:15-23) to realize the tremendous worth of their religion, which they, belonging as they do to the second Christian generation, are in great danger of taking too lightly.

Whatever this rapid survey of the chief doctrines of Paul might have meant by itself, to churches without the collected letters of Paul, it must be clear that it would gain enormously in significance and power if those letters accompanied it. That the writer had the letters is certain. It is equally clear that he is the first man of whom we know who had them all in his possession. It is also a definite fact of literary history that the first literary reflections of Paul's letters and of Ephesians appear together, in Revelation and I Clement. These facts argue strongly for the origin of Ephesians as an introduction to the Pauline letters, on the occasion of their first publication.

Coleridge said of Ephesians that it embraced every doctrine of Christianity. Certainly this opening section does embrace almost every important doctrine of Pauline religion.

III
1:15-23

This is why I, for my part, since I have heard of your faith in the Lord Jesus and in all God's people, never cease to thank God for you when I mention you in my prayers. The God of our Lord Jesus Christ, the glorious Father, grant you the Spirit of wisdom and revelation through the knowledge of himself, enlightening the eyes of your mind so that you may know what the hope is to which he calls you, and how gloriously rich his inheritance is among God's people, and how surpassingly great his power is for us who believe; like the mighty strength he exerted in raising Christ from the dead, and seating him at his right hand in heaven, far above all hierarchies, authorities, powers, and dominions, and all titles that can be bestowed not only in this world but in the world to come. He has put everything under his feet and made him the indisputable head of the church, which is his body, filled by him who fills everything everywhere.

The Supreme Worth of Christianity

This exultant summary of Pauline Christianity is followed by a jubilant assertion of the superlative worth of the Christian faith, cast in the form of a paragraph of prayer and thanksgiving (1:15-23). The writer rejoices in the spread of Christianity, and in the growing faith of Christians in Jesus and in one another.[1] He prays that God by the Spirit may so enlighten them that they may come to appreciate their glorious religion and its vast possibilities, through the power of God, which has exalted Christ above all spiritual beings and made him the head of the church, and which now sustains them. Obviously suggested by passages like Rom. 1:8 f., I Cor. 1:4 f., Phil. 1:3 f., Col. 1:3 f., I Thess. 1:2 f., II Thess. 1:3 f., the prayer is shaped

---

[1] That this is the meaning of this much-discussed passage is shown by the close parallel to it in Philemon, vs. 5, from which it is evidently derived.

into an assertion of the extraordinary worth of the Christian religion, which Christians are evidently in danger of forgetting. It is not so much logical as emotional—full of exultant, ecstatic feeling.

The timeliness of this appeal, in a day when Christians of the second generation were losing the early enthusiasm of the movement, is shown, we repeat, by the similar appeal in the Revelation and in Hebrews, both works of the last decade of the century. It is no formal or perfunctory utterance but a message definitely demanded by the state of Christianity in those times. Its pertinence in the days of Paul, when Christian faith was in its first eager, overflowing phase, would be far less. Indeed it would fit in any age of the church better than in the lifetime of Paul himself. Indifference and coldness were not the failings of primitive Christianity. But by the time Hebrews was written, they had begun to appear, and that epistle was written directly to meet them.[2] This is precisely the approach of Ephesians. To Christians everywhere the writer sends this appeal to value their great Christian inheritance at its true worth.

The reference to the readers' "faith in all God's people" (vs. 15), suggested by Philemon, verse 5, and much debated by interpreters, falls into a natural perspective in a time when mutual confidence and understanding is seen to be a necessary protection against the inroads of the sects. It accords admirably with the writer's later injunction to "pray for all God's people" (6:19). This mutual interest and appreciation must bind the churches together, in a time when the sectarian danger is coming seriously to threaten them.

---

[2] Even the church at Ephesus had "left its first love" (Rev. 2:4).

What the people addressed in the epistle need is seen to be Wisdom, Revelation, Knowledge, and Enlightenment (vss. 17, 18). These are Pauline words, but they are here gathered into an un-Pauline group. We feel that we are on our way to the Johannine view of religion, with its emphasis upon light, knowledge, and truth. This way of taking Pauline materials and making of them something that goes beyond Paul is characteristic of the writer of Ephesians, and very naturally, since he is making a bridge between his own age and the Pauline literature that he is introducing to it. The idea of religion as Enlightenment characterizes Hebrews also (6:4, 32), and baptism was spoken of as Enlightenment by the time of the Ephesian convert Justin, in the second quarter of the second century.

The insistence upon the supreme worth of Christianity, as beyond other faiths, and of Christ as beyond other Lords, indicates a time when Christianity has begun to be conscious of the rivalry of other religions, such as the Mystery cults. It belongs to a period of reflection. There are other faiths, and other masters; how do ours stand, in comparison with these? This is just the interest of Hebrews, which argues the vast superiority of the new faith to even the noblest of the old religions. Ephesians treats this matter with exuberant confidence: To what a hope he has called us! How gloriously rich is the inheritance! How surpassingly great is God's power for us to believe! Christ is far above all hierarchies, powers, dominions, and titles! He is the indisputable head of the church![3] This exuberant lan-

[3] The thought of the divine fulness, the Pleroma, so central in Colossians is not greatly emphasized in Ephesians; instead of retaining its technical sense, the word is adapted to uses nearer to the writer's immediate interest, which has little to do with the old Colossian speculations (1:10, 23; 3:19; 4:13). Colossians was especially concerned with Christ's relation to the universe; Ephesians is principally interested in his relation to the Church.

guage is of course in part liturgical; but it is also definitely demanded by that element in second-generation Christianity, which does not know how to prize the faith it has inherited. In a world so full of such people today it should not be difficult for us to envisage the situation here implied. The writer says these things, not as Scott suggests, "for his own satisfaction" (p. 123), but because the times cryingly demanded that they be said.

It is extraordinary how lifeless and mechanical most treatments of Ephesians make the epistle. All the steam and energy seem to evaporate from it, leaving only the mechanical parts. This is a sure sign that such interpreters have not penetrated the mind of the writer, and do not perceive what he is aiming at, or what animated him.

He is in fact seeking to do just what the writer of Hebrews, shortly after, attempted in a different way. He is trying to make a generation that has inherited Christianity appreciate its inheritance. To a Christian church in grave danger of misprizing its inherited faith, he points out in enthusiastic terms and in expansive language its beauties and glories. It is this feeling that controls the second main division of the letter (1:15—2:10).

It had already dawned upon the writer of Luke-Acts that Christianity was not a small local affair, but was swinging into that tremendous race with the great older religions for the supremacy of the ancient world. With those faiths the writer of Ephesians boldly challenges comparison. The power of God, the supremacy of Christ, his relation to the Church—these are matters Christians would do well to think upon, for they mark their faith as supremely true. The writer knows but one church—the Church Universal, the body of Christ himself. Paul himself occasionally uses the word "church" in this way; the writer of Ephesians uses it in no way but this. Indeed it is not too much to say that he is careful to use it in no other sense. Paul's frequent plural, "the churches," is impossible for him, so solicitous is he for the unity of the Church, which in his day is so seriously threatened.

All this prayer for the enlightenment of the readers and for their spiritual wisdom takes on a redoubled force if this letter is the introduction to the newly gathered Pauline letters. They will need some insight and understanding to read those letters, but if they can be enlightened and spiritually prepared to read them, what a spiritual treasure they will unfold! What a reinforcement for the religious life! What an arsenal of Christian truth! The early gospels were easy reading. They made no such demand upon the reader's intellectual powers as Paul's letters did, and still do. The immensely greater popularity of the gospels then, in the Middle Ages, and now, is in part due to this quality.

Paul's letters were harder. But how repaying! Their discoverer and collector had found that out. And if Christians everywhere could receive the Spirit of wisdom and revelation, and have the eyes of their minds enlightened, they might gain from these old letters some idea of the splendor of the Christian hope, the glory and richness of the divine inheritance, God's surpassing power for believers; and all that Paul has to tell them, if they will but hear him.

The ancient reader who began to unroll the first edition of the letters of Paul, and found what we call Ephesians at the beginning of them, would find in this passage not simply liturgical satisfaction, nor a sounding rhetorical panegyric upon the glories of Christianity, but a challenge to accept the enlightenment of the Spirit and delve deeply into the book he held in his hands, to find in it the religious values it might disclose. These verses do in a happier way what is so trenchantly essayed in Heb. 5:11—6:3.

IV

2:1–10

You also were dead because of the offenses and sins in the midst of which you once lived under the control of the present age of the world, and the master-spirit of the air, who is still at work among the disobedient. We all lived among them once, indulging our physical cravings and obeying the impulses of our lower nature and its thoughts, and by nature we were doomed to God's wrath like other men. But God is so rich in mercy that because of the great love he had for us, he made us, dead as we were through our offenses, live again with the Christ. It is by his mercy that you have been saved. And he raised us with Christ, and through our union with Christ Jesus made us sit down with him in heaven, to show the incomparable wealth of his mercy throughout the ages to come by his goodness to us through Christ Jesus. For it is by his mercy that you have been saved through faith. It is not by your own action, it is the gift of God. It has not been earned, so that no one can boast of it. For he has made us, creating us through our union with Christ Jesus for the life of goodness which God had predestined us to live.

The Christian Experience a New Life, Through God's Mercy

The Christian experience, the letter goes on, is a new life, through the power of God (2:1–10). The exultant review of the blessings of the Christian salvation, as understood by Paul, is resumed. The death and resurrection of Christ (1:20) suggest the Christian resurrection from the death of sin to the life of goodness. From their old deadness and bondage they have been delivered and raised to a better life with him, and transported to his side in heaven, by the unspeakable mercy of God. Their experience will stand for ages as a magnificent example of the greatness of God's mercy. The Christian is a new creation.

Paul saw a good deal of difference between the moral backgrounds of Jew and heathen, as the opening chapters of Romans clearly show. That difference is obliterated here (vs. 3), for "our" sins are not different from "yours" (vss. 1, 2). Indeed, the sins here described as "ours," that is, the Jews', are just what Paul described as characteristically heathen in Romans, chapter 1. This is the sign manual of a Greek hand, and the mark of a later time, when the difference between heathen and Jewish ethical backgrounds was no longer keenly felt in the church. The writer is a Greek Christian; in this verse the disguise slips for a moment, and he acknowledges his own heathen past, or at least extraction.

The resemblance to Romans is very striking: Universal depravity, heathen and Jewish, terminated by the sheer mercy of God, who through Christ has delivered us all, through no merit of our own. The contacts in order and in detail with Romans, chapters 1–3, are unmistakable. Lock remarks, in commenting on this passage, that chapters 1 and 2 "are in the spirit of Rom. 1–5." And in fact 2:1–10 read almost like a summary of Romans, chapters 1–5.

The satanic figure of II Thess. 2:3–9 is no longer thought of as portending the messianic Parousia but as the dominating force of the old evil life and age, from which the Christian has been delivered.[1] The messianic drama of Thessa-

---

[1] "The master-spirit of the air, who is still at work [ἐνεργοῦντος] among the disobedient" is a reminiscence of the Antichrist of II Thess. 2:3–10: "The embodiment of disobedience [ἀνομίας] . . . . . For disobedience is already secretly at work, ... The other's appearance, by the contrivance [κατ' ἐνέργειαν] of Satan, will be full of power . . . . and full of wicked deception for men who are going to destruction, because they refused to love the truth and be saved." Other words for disobedience—ἀνομία, ἀδικία—are used here steadily in place of ἀπείθια, but the influence of the passage seems unmistakable. Note also the "misleading influence," ἐνέργειαν πλάνης (vs. 11). The expression οἱ υἱοὶ τῆς ἀπειθίας used here

lonians has manifestly faded from its old vividness and sharpness.

The seating of the believer with Christ in heaven (vs. 6) is also a development upon Pauline ideas, expressed in Col. 3:3: "Your life now lies hidden with Christ in God," anticipating the Christian's destiny as already assured. It suggests the representations in Revelation, and, more inwardly, the strong doctrine of the Christian's union with Christ in the Gospel of John.

The fulness of expression, approaching redundancy, continues to reveal the liturgical character of the epistle. The combination "offenses and sins" (vs. 1), not found in Paul, the "incomparable wealth of his mercy" (vs. 7), and the difficult repetition of "by his mercy you have been saved" (vss. 5, 8) are probably to be thus explained.

---

is repeated in 5:6; Paul employs a more direct expression: οἱ ἀπειθοῦντες (Rom. 15:31). Yet compare his υἱὸς τῆς ἀπωλείας in II Thess. 2:3. Not only the thoughts then but all the materials of the expression of Eph. 2:2b are supplied by this striking paragraph in II Thessalonians. The writer of Ephesians has simply made them his own, as is his wont.

V
2:11-22

So remember that you were once physically heathen, and called uncircumcised by those who called themselves circumcised, though only physically, by human hands. At that time you had no connection with Christ, you were aliens to the commonwealth of Israel, and strangers to the agreements about God's promise; with no hope and no God in all the world. But now through your union with Christ Jesus you who were once far away have through the blood of Christ been brought near. For he is himself our peace. He has united the two divisions, and broken down the barrier that kept us apart, and through his human nature put an end to the feud between us, and abolished the Law with its rules and regulations, in order to make peace and create out of the two parties one new man by uniting them with himself, and to kill the feud between them with his cross and in one body reconcile them both to God with it. He came with the good news of peace for you who were far away and for those who were near; for it is through him that we both with one Spirit are now able to approach the Father. So you are no longer foreigners or strangers, but you are fellow-citizens of God's people and members of his family. You are built upon the apostles and prophets as your foundation, and Christ Jesus himself is the cornerstone. Through him every part of the building is closely united and grows into a temple sacred through its relation to the Lord, and you are yourselves built up into a dwelling for God through the Spirit.

Christ's Death Opens the Greeks' Way to God

Greek Christianity is next reminded of its former dark estate, in contrast with its present happy condition (2:11-22). Out of its Christless heathen past it had been brought by the death of Christ into full reconciliation and sonship, and full citizenship, with every right and privilege anyone could claim, in apostles, prophets, and Christ; in the building of God.

Paul wrote to the Romans, "But it is to you who are of the heathen that I am speaking" (11:13). Ephesians speaks of Greek Christians as no longer heathen: "Remember that you were once physically heathen. "Why do they need to be reminded of this? Is it to prepare them to understand what Paul says on the subject, and the way he speaks to their immediate predecessors? It would seem that a time has been reached when Greek Christians no longer think of themselves as "heathen," τὰ ἔθνη, but as Christians, in contrast with Jews on the one hand and heathen on the other. How well this fits with the period of Luke-Acts is very clear. It is on the way to the idea of the Christians as a new race, that appears in the *Apology* of Aristides, half a century later.

It would appear that when the epistle is written, all Christians (see 1:1) are ex-heathen. They are no longer thought of as "physically heathen," τὰ ἔθνη ἐν σαρκί; they only remember that they were so once. Have they then been circumcised? Yes, with the circumcision of the heart described in Rom. 2:28, 29: "Real circumcision is a matter of the heart, a spiritual, not a literal, thing." This is a matter of the greatest importance for date and occasion. The Jew has dwindled out of the picture, as far as the Church is concerned. God's people, the saints, of 1:1, everywhere are Gentiles. There is, for the writer at least, no Jewish Christianity any more.

The manner of speaking, "Remember that you were once physically heathen," strikingly resembles Heb. 10:32, "But you must remember those early days when after you had received the light you had to go through a great struggle with persecution." Both passages imply a long

Christian retrospect, and come from the same period late in the first century when men were beginning to see religious value in such reflections.

The Greeks have somehow come to replace the Jews as the heirs of their religious heritage. "But now through your union with Christ Jesus you who were once far away have through the blood of Christ been brought near." The idea of the Jew and Greek as united in Christ recalls Gal. 3:28, "There is no room for 'Jew' and 'Greek,'" and Col. 3:11: "What matters is not 'Greek' and 'Jew.'" But the form in which it is put points to a time late in the first century, when the subject was no longer a matter of heated controversy. This is rather a calm retrospect of the old conflict which had been so bitter in the time of Paul.

Why then bring it up at all? For two reasons: to make the frequent vehement references to the matter in Paul's letters intelligible and acceptable to the Greek readers of them; and to bring home to them the importance of unity in their own day against the sects. To understand Paul's letters, they must indeed remember that they were themselves once physically heathen, and the heirs and successors of the people whose rights in the new faith he had so strenuously championed. To be sure, the disunion of the readers' day is not between Greeks and Jews, but between Greeks of different sects; but it is the old unity for which Christ came and suffered that is still needed.

To say that Christ has "abolished the Law, with its rules and regulations" (vs. 15) is a strong contrast to Paul's words in Rom. 3:31: "Is this using faith to overthrow law? Far from it. This confirms the Law." Yet in Rom. 10:4 Paul does say, "Christ marks the termination of the

Law," and 7:4 contains a similar idea: "So you, in turn, my brothers, in the body of Christ have become dead as far as the Law is concerned." The thought of the passage thus has precedents in Paul, but clearly goes farther than Paul would have done. Here, as often in the letter, the writer puts an idea of Paul into a statement perhaps suggested by Paul but never so strongly put by him.

Striking elements in this paragraph confirm a date late in the first century for the letter. The barrier in the temple which shut Gentiles out of the Court of the Women was destroyed at the fall of Jerusalem and the destruction of the temple in A.D. 70. It could hardly have been spoken of at an earlier date as broken down. It is its actual destruction that suggests its figurative use here.

The representation of the Church as made up wholly of Gentiles (2:11) makes the late date of the letter still clearer, and taken in conjunction with the encyclical address of 1:1, leaves no room for Christians of Jewish blood. All are of heathen stock. This cannot have been the case much before A.D. 90.

The interpretation of the death of Christ, too, as breaking down the barrier between Jew and Greek and admitting the Greek to full rights in the great religious inheritance of Judaism is far removed from the earlier understandings of it. The death of Christ, it is now perceived, has enfranchised Greek Christianity.

The conception of the Universal Church (the only sense, we recall, in which the epistle uses the word "church") as built upon the apostles and prophets as its foundation is also far removed from primitive Christian forms of thought. With them, Christ was the foundation, as Paul puts it in I Cor. 3:11: "For no one can lay any other foundation than the one that is laid, that is, Jesus Christ himself." On the other hand, the idea of the apostles as the foundation of the Church comes out very strongly in the Revelation, the first book of Christian literature to be written after the appearance of Ephesians and the Pauline corpus of letters. It had in fact just been clearly brought out by the Book of Acts. The idea is as natural and established for the nineties as it is strange and out of place much earlier.

Efforts to interpret this paragraph to fit an earlier date therefore find it full of strange difficulties, which immediately melt away or become full of welcome significance when its true date and occasion are accepted.

VI
3:1–13

Paul in His Writings Declares the Greeks' Full Rights in Christianity

This is why I, Paul, whom Jesus the Christ has made a prisoner for the sake of you heathen—if at least you have heard how I dealt with the mercy of God that was given me for you, and how the secret was made known to me by revelation, as I have just briefly written. As you read that, you will be able to understand the insight I have into the secret of the Christ (which in past ages was not disclosed to mankind as fully as it has now been revealed through the Spirit to his holy apostles and prophets) that through union with Christ Jesus the heathen are fellow-heirs with the Jews, belong to the same body and share the promise with them, through the good news for which I became a worker by virtue of the gift of God's mercy which by the exercise of his power he has given me. To me, the very least of all his people, this favor has been given, of preaching to the heathen the inexhaustible wealth of the Christ, and making clear how the secret purpose is to be worked out which has been hidden away for ages in God the creator of all things, so that the many-sided wisdom of God may now through the church be made known to the rulers and authorities in heaven, fulfilling the eternal purpose which God carried out in Christ Jesus our Lord. Through union with him and through faith in him, we have courage to approach God with confidence. So I ask that what I am having to suffer for your sake may not make me lose heart, for it does you honor.

The strongly autobiographical and self-commendatory tone of the next paragraph of the epistle (3:1–13) has naturally perplexed commentators. Moule calls it a digression. Burton, viewing the letter as part doctrinal and part practical, considers it a transition from one to the other. Scott speaks of it as a "personal digression," one of the "parentheses" that interrupt chapters 1–3. Dibelius takes a similar view.

The commendation to Greek Christians of what Paul has written (vss. 3, 4) is passed over lightly by most interpreters. At best, they dismiss it as a reference to what has already been written (and read) in chapters 1 and 2 of this epistle (Abbott, Scott). The old practice of making verse 3 a parenthesis (King James, followed by Moffatt, who makes the parenthesis include vss. 3*b*–5) tends further to conceal this vitally important clue to the origin and intent of the epistle.

The extraordinary claim to special insight into the long-concealed secret of the Christ Scott feels it necessary to defend against charges of arrogance and self-admiration, though his parallels from Thackeray and Lord Byron might as fairly be taken as proving the very opposite.[1]

It is the main purpose of these pages to show that this paragraph, instead of being a transition, digression, or parenthesis, is the point of chief emphasis in the letter; the thing its writer especially wishes to say, and for a time emerges from his liturgical mood to state in plain words.

The emphatic disjunctive way in which the paragraph 3:1–13 opens—"This is why I, Paul"—calls attention to something of importance that is coming, an impression that is heightened by its anacolouthic form; it remains incomplete. It is in fact Paul himself who is now presented, after the summary of Pauline doctrine, and the rhapsody over the worth of the Christian religion, as a martyr to his devotion to the Greek mission, of whom they may be supposed to have heard, and who has previously written of the secret revealed to him—that the heathen fully share the religious inheritance of the Jews. This is the great dis-

---

[1] Scott, *Colossians, Philemon, Ephesians,* p. 184.

closure. This is a very different idea of the "secret" from that in Colossians, although the same word is used. To declare this secret to the heathen has been the vocation of Paul, and has now become the mission of the Church, which is henceforth to serve as the medium of God's wisdom to the world, and so to carry out God's eternal purpose. Christ has opened the Greek's way to God. Paul himself is a martyr to the cause of the Greek mission. His imprisonment and death are for the heathen.

This is not all. For this rapid picture of Paul, imprisoned for his missionary work among the heathen, contains one important touch not included even in the sketch of him in the Acts: he was not simply a missionary and a martyr; he was a *writer* on the secret of Christ; a writer of extraordinary insight and power, who now commends to them what he has written as proof of this unique understanding of the mystery so long concealed. In short, in this passage Paul is introduced for the first time as a *writer*, whose works will edify the Church. For they embody his great disclosure, that the Jewish religious inheritance belongs to the Greeks. Here in this paragraph the writings of Paul are introduced and recommended to the Greek Church.

The value of the paragraph is clear. It is to reintroduce Paul to any who may not know Acts. To any who do, it is to identify the author of the letters as the missionary hero of Acts; to describe his function in connection with Greek Christians; their prisoner, their missionary, their writer, their martyr. It was his life-work to convey to them the secret of Christ. They may still read that secret in his letters, below!

Here emerges the purpose of Ephesians as the Introduction to the collected letters. Paul's relation to Greek Christianity (their prisoner, missionary, martyr) justifies Greek interest in his collected letters; in company with which unmistakably Ephesians first made its appearance. The readers of Ephesians are expected to read Paul's letters, and find in them, as the writer of Ephesians had done, the proof of his deep understanding of the Christian faith.

So understood, the writer's admiration for Paul's extraordinary insight becomes perfectly natural and unobjectionable. The writer of the epistle is the first man of whom we know who read all the Pauline letters, and he may well have been impressed, as men still are, with the apostle's penetration and religious understanding. He would certainly wish all Greek Christians to share with him the great religious inheritance contained in the nine Pauline letters, and would feel confident that they would gain greatly from reading them. Other interpretations find verses 3 and 4 awkward and troublesome. If he is simply referring to chapters 1 and 2, which the readers must just have read, to reach this point in the epistle, why must they be told to read them again? If chapters 1 and 2 are so edifying, the reader must already be edified. Or is it only by re-reading them that he can gain the edification they have to give? Chrysostom was certainly right in thinking that the reference is to some other writing of Paul's. The language unmistakably points to a *later* reading of an *earlier* writing of Paul's. And what could be more natural, if the collected Pauline letters followed? It is to them that the writer refers the interested reader, whom he has already introduced to Paul's leading religious positions, in chapters 1 and 2.

The verb used in verse 3, προγράφω, must of course be closely

THE OCCASION AND MEANING 43

scrutinized. It is frequently used in papyrus documents in the participle, in the sense of "before mentioned, above mentioned"; but is also used in referring to a previous letter, as in Oxyrhynchus Papyri No. 291 (A.D. 25–26): "I wrote you before to be firm and demand payment, until I am well enough to come."[2] This instance from the first century establishes the usage proposed above for verse 3.

Some very definite things in this paragraph strike the eye. Paul is the missionary hero, as in Acts. He is recognized as the founder of the Greek mission, as there. His sufferings for that cause, that is, of course, his martyrdom, have become the glory of Greek Christianity. All this is the manifest product of time and reflection.

The holy apostles and prophets are introduced (vs. 5) in a way altogether unlike Paul or his time, but entirely natural and appropriate after the appearance of Acts and before that of Revelation, which speaks of saints, apostles, and prophets (18:20). Furthermore, the *inspiration* of the holy apostles and prophets is here announced; a natural inference from Luke-Acts, indeed, but difficult to push farther back.

The Church is henceforth to be the medium of God's wisdom (vs. 10), succeeding to the exalted function of apostles and prophets, a highly developed doctrine of the Church.

As Paul's leading doctrines have been distinguished (chap. 1) his letters also now emerge from a generation of obscurity to take their permanent and commanding place in Christian literature. It is certain that the writer of Ephesians had and used every one of the nine accepted letters of

---

[2] καὶ προέγραψά σοι ἀνδραγαθεῖν καὶ ἀπαιτεῖν μέχρι ὑγιαίνων παραγένωμαι (Oxyrhynchus Papyri, II, 291).

Paul. It is also clear that he is the first writer known to have done this. It is further established that he wrote his letter to present Pauline Christianity to Greek Christians everywhere and to arouse them to a sense of the immeasurable worth of their religion. What could be more natural than to commend to them those very letters of Paul which the writer himself has found so inspiring? It is precisely this that the writer of Ephesians does in this central paragraph of his letter. Other explanations of it lag and falter. But taken at its face value, it becomes at once luminous.

The publication of the Pauline letters must have been a perfectly conscious and definite act on the part of someone in the early Church. Pliny's first letter tells how Septicius had urged him to publish his own collected letters and thus led him to do so. The Revelation shows that the Ephesian circle before the end of the first century knew something about circulating a Christian pamphlet among the churches. By the early years of the tenth decade everything was ready. Luke-Acts reflects a literary interest and attitude—the consciousness of sources, written and oral, the planning of the work in two volumes, the preface, the dedication, the interest in Christian poesy. That work had also brought forward the figure of Paul, the hero and martyr of the Greek mission, and presented to the churches an inimitable picture of him. A revival of interest in Paul must have resulted. Nothing could be more natural than that under its influence someone already acquainted with one or two letters of his (Colossians, Philemon) should have instituted a search among the Pauline churches mentioned in Acts—Galatia, Philippi, Thessalonica, Corinth, Rome—for such letters of his as survived in their church chests, preserved probably to be read in church on the anniversary of his martyrdom. The letters, regarded by their first recipients as valuable only for the time and situation each dealt with, were naturally neglected. It was only when combined that their surpassing religious worth appeared. Here again the whole was more than the sum of all the parts. Upon their collector therefore first burst the full great value of the Pauline corpus. Under its exalting influence he writes his summary, indorsement, and introduction of them, and puts them forth, as a great literary heritage from the founder of Greek Christianity.

All this lies behind verses 3 and 4. The collection and publication of Paul's letters was an event in early Christian literature quite comparable with the writing of any one of them. It importantly affected all subsequent Christian literature. That it should be somewhere definitely reflected in that literature is altogether natural and probable. Certainly the first document to show acquaintance with Pauline letters may be expected to allude to them, especially if its writer is familiar with them all. It would be extremely artificial of its writer to do otherwise. So to the nine letters to which he owes so much, and from which almost every line of his own letter is drawn, he points his readers for further evidence of the religious genius of the apostle Paul.

Coming to this position independently, I find great satisfaction in the observation of Juelicher, in the fifth edition of his *Introduction*, that on most accounts the natural explanation of the purpose and aim of Ephesians is that it was to serve as introduction to a collection of Pauline letters (pp. 127, 128). It was in fact only what he considered its excessive use of Colossians that prevented him from adopting this explanation and led him to declare the problem of the origin of Ephesians still unsolved. But if the writer were or had been a Colossian Christian, or an Ephesian who in traveling about Asia Minor had become acquainted with Colossians and possessed himself of a copy of it, this fuller familiarity with it would be explained. It would be artificial to assume that the writer must have become acquainted with all the Pauline letters simultaneously. If he was also the collector of them, he must have known some of them before he did others. He had to begin somewhere. His saturation with Colossians only means that that was the letter he had known longest and so knew best. Moreover, while he uses it most, he just as certainly used every one of the nine accepted letters. The author's abundant use of Colossians is in short not a difficulty; it is rather a clue, of the utmost value, to the *Asian origin* of the collection. "It is not yet settled," said Johannes Weiss, in his *Urchristentum*, page 534, "whether the author of the Letter to the Ephesians is not the very collector of the Pauline Corpus."

To these acute suggestions I would give hearty assent. The author was in all probability the collector of the Pauline corpus; and Ephesians was written to introduce the collected letters to the Christian world.

VII
3:14-21

For this reason I kneel before the Father from whom every family in heaven or on earth takes its name, and beg him out of his wealth of glory to strengthen you mightily through his Spirit in your inner nature and through your faith to let Christ in his love make his home in your hearts. Your roots must be deep and your foundations strong, so that you and all God's people may be strong enough to grasp what breadth, length, height, and depth mean, and to understand Christ's love, so far beyond our understanding, so that you may be filled with the very fulness of God. To him who by the exertion of his power within us can do unutterably more than all we ask or imagine, be glory through the church and through Christ Jesus through all generations forever and ever. Amen.

The Grandeur of the Experience of Christ's Love

In a second prayerful appeal, built up to a noble doxology as its climax (3:14-21), the writer urges upon his readers, the Greek Christians, the inner life of love. He would have them grasp the full magnitude of their salvation, what breadth, length, height, depth, really mean, that coveted divine Pleroma—fulness—with which, through the understanding of Christ's love, they must be filled. Of course that love is really far beyond our understanding, and this superlative is echoed in the stately doxology, in the power of God within us, which can do unutterably more than all we ask or imagine. The Church Universal, which has been shown (vs. 10) to be the channel of his wisdom to men, is to be the channel of man's praise to him through all the generations—a striking assertion of the liturgical function of the Church.

No one can fail to feel the religious worth and the liturgical power of this prayer. Once more the writer seeks to awaken his Christian brethren to the supreme value and tremendous possibilities of their faith, to its magnificent ideals and hopes. It is this combination of deep religious insight with lofty liturgical expression that constitutes the distinctive genius of Ephesians. Robinson calls this a prayer for knowledge, and the emphasis is still on comprehension. The writer's fear here, as in 1:15-23, is that Christians have lost the true appreciation of the immense worth of their religion, and he constantly seeks by every means in his power to reawaken them to it.

The writer's constant use of Church to mean the Church Universal leads him to use the more intimate word "family," πατριά, for the little individual groups of believers scattered over the empire. Paul himself in Gal. 6:10 spoke of those who belonged to the family of the faith, and the writer had already said (2:19), "You are of the household [οἰκεῖοι] of God." This naturally prepares the way for his reference to the Church as a family of God. We cannot prove this to have been a Mysteries term for a local group, but such groups were sometimes headed by a Father, πατήρ, and I cannot doubt that this is the meaning of the much-discussed πατριά of verse 15. The local Christian groups, too, have their πατήρ, the universal Father.[1] The word has proved an enigma for commentators. Scott some-

---

[1] The highest of the seven orders in Mithraism was the Father. Paul speaks of himself as having been a father to the church at Corinth (I Cor. 4:15), and Matt. 23:9 seems to refer to practices of the Mystery religions: "You must not call anyone on earth your father, for you have only one father, your heavenly Father." In the Martyrdom of Polycarp, 12:2, the people cry, "This is the teacher of Asia, the father of the Christians." See also Ignatius, Ephesians 6. The Mystery groups were some of them brotherhoods,

what obscurely says that all races are conceived as calling themselves by the name of God (p. 194)—a very alien and dubious observation to find a place in the epistle. Even Dibelius sees in the sentence only a rhetorical way of asserting the fatherhood of God. But the logic of the connection seems clear: Christ has opened the Greek's way to God; he may now approach him with confidence. For this reason the writer prays that the Father, from whom every church family in the world derives its life, may build up their inner lives in faith and love.

The mention of every family in heaven or on earth recalls attention to the universal, encyclical character of the letter, already indicated in 1:1. This direct relation of the individual church to God himself is the sanction of the unity of the great Church Universal. John later found that sanction in the individual's relation to Christ; in union with him. Ignatius about the same time found it in harmony with the local bishop. Ephesians here finds it in the local church's relation to God; he is its Father.

The reference to families in heaven is difficult for every interpretation of the passage, but less so for the one proposed than for others. The Revelation places in the hands of Christ the seven stars which are the guardian angels of the seven churches, and the martyrs are thought of as standing before the throne and the Lamb. Stephen in the Acts dies saying, "Lord Jesus, receive my spirit!" The martyrs in I Peter are to intrust their souls to a Creator who

---

those of Dionysus, for example. Christians are also so spoken of in I Pet. 2:17: "Love the brotherhood." From the point of view of God's fatherhood, they might quite as naturally be spoken of as "families," πατριαί, which seems to be the unmistakable sense here.

is faithful. All this belongs to a different atmosphere from the Pauline eschatology, and much nearer to that implied in families of believers in heaven. The Descent into Hades described in chapter 4 looks in a similar direction. It seems clear that the ideas of a future life reflected in these later books are much nearer to the Johannine picture of a hospitable Father's house awaiting the Christian than to the Pauline eschatology with its long-deferred final judgment.

The Church Universal is thus seen to consist of all the countless families of believers, militant or triumphant, and the passage becomes an almost exact parallel of that in 2:21, 22, where the growing temple which God is to dwell in has its every part. To the πᾶσα οἰκοδομή of 2:21 the πᾶσα πατριά of 3:15 corresponds.

The placing of the doxology at this point in the letter follows the Pauline-letter type, the Thessalonian letters with the benediction after the main part of the letter, and Romans with its exultant outburst at the end of the great argument (8:31–39).

As we survey the paragraph from the point of view of date, we are struck with its developed liturgical form. The liturgical *interest* of Ephesians (5:14, 19, 20), which Harnack denied, is far less than its strikingly liturgical *character*, which is so warmly affirmed even by advocates of its Pauline origin, and which really binds it inseparably to the age of Luke-Acts, the Revelation, Hebrews, and I Clement.

Again, the encyclical interest of the letter, reflected in the "every family" of verse 15, with "all God's people," verse 18, and "the Church" Universal, verse 21, recalls us to the address of 1:1, and the times when an encyclical address to Christians everywhere could be thought of.

The Pleroma, or fulness, is coming to have an ethical rather than a cosmic sense; as also in 4:13; and the eschatology—"every family in heaven"—is taking on Greek forms in place of Jewish. At every point both the manner and the matter of the section exhibit the atmosphere of the tenth decade.

VIII
4:1-16

So I, the prisoner for the Lord's sake, appeal to you to live lives worthy of the summons you have received; with perfect humility and gentleness, with patience, bearing with one another lovingly. Make every effort to maintain the unity of the Spirit through the tie of peace. There is but one body and one Spirit, just as there is but one hope that belongs to the summons you received. There is but one Lord, one faith, one baptism, one God and Father of all, who is above us all, pervades us all, and is within us all. But each one of us has been given mercy in Christ's generous measure. So it says,

Christians Must Be United Against the Sects

"When he went up on high, he led a host of captives,
And gave gifts to mankind."

What does "he went up" mean, except that he had first gone down to the under parts of the earth? It is he who went down who has also gone up above all the heavens, to fill the universe. And he has given us some men as apostles, some as prophets, some as missionaries, some as pastors and teachers, in order to fit his people for the work of service, for building the body of Christ, until we all attain unity in faith, and in the knowledge of the Son of God, and reach mature manhood, and that full measure of development found in Christ. We must not be babies any longer, blown about and swung around by every wind of doctrine through the trickery of men with their ingenuity in inventing error. We must lovingly hold to the truth and grow up into perfect union with him who is the head—Christ himself. For it is under his control that the whole system, adjusted and united by each ligament of its equipment, develops in proportion to the functioning of each particular part, and so builds itself up through love.

Numberless interpreters of Paul have declared that his letter-plan is to deal first with doctrinal and then with practical matters. The writer to the Ephesians was clearly the first to perceive this and to follow it. Broadly speaking, chapters 4-6 are devoted to urging upon the believers a better life.

The Paul whose sufferings for Greek Christianity have given him such a right to address them appeals to them to live in harmony. The specific need of the hour is reunion against the encroachments of the sects, and the writer begins with a great appeal for Christian unity (4:1-16). He has already shown that Christ died to make us one (2:13-18); now they must make their lives respond to this great challenge. They must realize in their lives this new unity (vss. 3-6), attended, of course, with diversity of gifts (vss. 7-10) and of function (vss. 11-13)—over against the sects (vs. 14) and under the headship of Christ (vss. 15, 16).

The word "unity" (ἑνότης) here makes its first and only appearances in the New Testament (vss. 3, 13), and the idea is built up with tremendous power in the sentences that follow its introduction. Why should there be sects in the body of Christ? He has but one body. There is but one Spirit. One hope lies before us all. There is but one Lord, one faith, one baptism, one God and Father of all. It hardly needs the explicit evidence of verse 14 to show that we are in the presence of the schismatic movements to which Acts refers (20:29, 30), against which the Revelation warns (2:6, 15, etc.), and with which John and Ignatius later dealt. Against these the Church Universal must maintain the glorious unity implied in its fundamental constitution, as the body of Christ.

Gifts indeed may vary; they are Christ's gifts to his Church, sent from his exalted position to which he went up after he had first gone down to the under parts of the earth. This first appearance of the Descent into Hell is in strong contrast with Paul's meaning in Rom. 10:6, 7, although his words there evidently influenced the phraseology here. The Ascension, taught in Luke-Acts (Acts 1:9), has led to the doctrine of the Descensus ad Inferos (vss. 9, 10), soon reflected in I Pet. 4:6: "This is why the good news was preached to the dead also." In Descent and Ascension the writer finds imaginative confirmation of his idea that Christ fills the universe.

He returns to his discussion of the diverse gifts of the Church, in language strongly reminiscent of I Cor. 12:28; some are apostles, some prophets, some missionaries, some pastors—recalling Acts 20:28, where the corresponding verb occurs—and teachers. It is striking that the only words in this list not afforded by Paul are found, as noun or verb, in the Acts, 20:28; 21:8. All these work for one purpose: the development of the body of Christ, that all may attain unity, in faith and the knowledge of Christ, and arrive at full Christian stature.

The chief danger to such ideal unity lies in the sects already described in Acts 20:30, and later opposed in Revelation, the letters of Ignatius, and John. The way to it lies in union with Christ. Such union is the only way to sound and worthy spiritual development.

Three things in this paragraph strongly suggest a date near the end of the first century:

1. The developed and specialized church offices and functions: to the primitive apostles, prophets, and teachers are now added missionaries ("evangelists") and pastors ("shepherds"). "Evangelist" meets us first in the Acts, though the corresponding verb is in Paul and the early gospels.

"Shepherd" in the Christian sense meets us first here, but is later dwelt upon in John, chapter 10. It is also applied to Christ in I Peter and in Hebrews, and was the name given by Hermas about 100 to his Mentor, The Angel of Repentance. The verb in the sense of "being a pastor to" is found in Acts 20:28.

2. The Descent into Hades has been developed out of the Ascension doctrine, which first appears in Acts. That this should have been stated by Paul in advance of the Ascension doctrine would be strange; doubly so in view of Rom. 10:6, 7, which look in the opposite direction. But the strangest thing about connecting the doctrine with Paul is the silence of Mark, Matthew, and Luke on the subject after him. On the other hand, if Ephesians was written soon after 90, it is natural to find the Descensus doctrine expressed so soon afterward in I Peter.[1]

3. The emphasis upon the unity of the Church against the sects is unmistakably the atmosphere of the closing years of the century. It is reflected shortly before in Acts 20:30 and shortly after in Revelation and still later in John and Ignatius, who uses ἑνότης eleven times. No such natural setting for it can be established in the sixties or in the eighties.

If there were nothing else in the epistle to point to a date late in the first century, these three striking features would suffice, they are so concrete, distinctive, and specific.

[1] Had the Descensus doctrine been put forth in a Pauline encyclical in the eighties, it could hardly have escaped the notice of Luke, writing about A.D. 90, and with his strong resurrection interest would certainly have attracted him. As a matter of fact, it is first echoed in I Peter and then in the Gospel of Peter, II Peter, and the Acts of Pilate.

IX
4:17—5:2

So what I mean and insist upon in the Lord's name is this: You must no longer live like the heathen, with their frivolity of mind and darkened understanding. They are estranged from the life of God be-

They Must Live the New, Upright Life

cause of the ignorance that exists among them and their obstinacy of heart, for they have become callous, and abandoned themselves to sensuality, greedily practicing every kind of vice. That is not the way you have been taught what Christ means, at least if you have really become acquainted with him and been instructed in him, and in union with him have been taught the truth as it is found in Jesus. You must lay aside with your former habits your old self which is going to ruin through its deceptive passions. You must adopt a new attitude of mind, and put on the new self which has been created in likeness to God, with all the uprightness and holiness that belong to the truth.

So you must lay aside falsehood and each tell his neighbor the truth, for we are parts of one another. Be angry, but do no sin. The sun must not go down upon your anger; you must not give the devil a chance. The man who stole must not steal any more; he must work with his hands at honest toil instead, so as to have something to share with those who are in need. No bad word must ever pass your lips, but only words that are good and suited to improve the occasion, so that they will be a blessing to those who hear them. You must not offend God's holy Spirit, with which you have been marked for the Day of Redemption. You must give up all bitterness, rage, anger, and loud, abusive talk, and all spite. You must be kind to one another, you must be tender-hearted, and forgive one another just as God through Christ has forgiven you. So follow God's example, like his dear children, and lead loving lives, just as Christ loved you and gave himself for you as a fragrant offering and sacrifice to God.

The life of union with Christ is a new life; not the old one of depravity and indulgence, but a new life of uprightness and likeness to God (4:17–24). Verses 17–19 read like a condensation of Rom. 1:18–32, with their dark picture of ancient heathen vice. The inner self must be transformed into a new attitude of mind. The figure of the "old man," ὁ παλαιὸς ἄνθρωπος, is clearly drawn from Col. 3:9, but here the contrasted picture is not the "young man," νέος, of Colossians, but the "new man," καινός. The word used in Ephesians is somewhat more suitable to the figure, though at the same time somewhat less bold and vivid, and was doubtless suggested by ἀνακαινούμενον in Col. 3:10; cf. Eph. 4:23.

The traits of the new life are rapidly and finely sketched: truthfulness, patience, honesty, decency, self-control, kindness, forgiveness, love (4:25—5:2). They remind us of the fruit of the Spirit, in Gal. 5:22, 23, but that is a mere list; here each is a little more fully presented.

The use of the word "devil" in verse 27 is a definite departure from Pauline usage; indeed, Mark never uses it. It appears first, in the New Testament books, in Matthew, then in Luke-Acts, then here, then in the Revelation, Hebrews, I Peter, etc. Even in the Pastorals, it is, except in one instance, used as a common noun, "slanderer."

The use of the "new man" for the "young man" of Paul's figure seems to imply reflection and improvement upon the earlier expression.

The studied pleonasm of "God's holy Spirit," τὸ πνεῦμα τὸ ἅγιον τοῦ θεοῦ, 4:30, is unmistakably and impressively liturgical.

The whole Christian public addressed in the epistle looks back upon a heathen way of life: "You must no longer live like the heathen" (vs. 17). The Church has become entirely Gentile, as the epistle repeatedly implies. All are converts from heathenism or the children of such converts. The Jewish element has disappeared from the Church.

X
5:3-21

But immorality or any form of vice or greed must not be so much as mentioned among you; that would not be becoming in God's people. There must be no indecency or foolish or scurrilous talk—all that is unbecoming. There should be thanksgiving instead. For you may be sure that no one who is immoral, or greedy for gain (for that is idolatry) can have any share in the Kingdom of Christ and God.

They Must Give up the Old Sins and Live in the New Light

Whatever anyone may say in the way of worthless arguments to deceive you, these are the things that are bringing God's anger down upon the disobedient. Therefore have nothing to do with them. For once you were sheer darkness, but now, as Christians, you are light itself. You must live like children of light, for light leads to perfect goodness, uprightness, and truth; you must make sure what pleases the Lord. Have nothing to do with the profitless doings of the darkness; expose them instead. For while it is degrading even to mention their secret practices, yet when anything is exposed by the light, it is made visible, and anything that is made visible is light. So it says,

"Wake up, sleeper!
Rise from the dead,
And Christ will dawn upon you!"

Be very careful, then, about the way you live. Do not act thoughtlessly, but like sensible men, and make the most of your opportunity, for these are evil times. So do not be foolish, but understand what the Lord's will is. Do not get drunk on wine, for that is profligacy, but be filled with the Spirit, and speak to one another in psalms, hymns, and sacred songs. Sing praise to God with all your hearts; always give thanks for everything to God our Father, as followers of our Lord Jesus Christ, and subordinate yourselves to one another out of reverence to Christ.

In a passage of supreme moral elevation, the writer continues to generalize and formulate the Christian ethic (5:3-21).

They must avoid the baser sins, immorality, vice, greed, indecency (vss. 3–5), and live in the new Light which has dawned upon them (vss. 6–14), undisturbed by sectarian sophistries. Christians are to have no fellowship with the holders of such views. The conception of religion as Light, so developed in the Gospel of John a few years later, implies a life of goodness, uprightness, and truth. The barren doings of the darkness, on the other hand, they must expose to the purifying influence of the Light. Some lines from an early hymn (rather than from the Apocalypse of Elijah), relate Christ to this life of Light; he is its dawning.

They must be wise, sensible, sober—finding their exhilaration not in wine, like the Dionysiac orgiasts, but in the presence of the Spirit, and expressing it in thanksgiving and religious song (vss. 15–21).

The schismatic peril reappears in verses 6 and 7. The old making light of sins of the flesh is now championed by a group within the Church, from whom true Christians are to hold aloof. But such people are not simply to be avoided, but exposed (vs. 11), when they fall into the sins of the old paganism. The writer quotes a baptismal hymn of the new hymnology just bursting into flower, and makes a revival use of it: Let these sleepers awake, and rise from their death in sin, to live in the Light of Christ.

The emphasis upon Christianity as Light has its early parallels in Paul, and its reflection in Matthew, but its full development is in John and Greek Christianity to which it was very congenial, and Justin in the middle of the second century described baptism as φωτισμός, "Enlightenment."[1]

The appeal to sing hymns and sacred songs together had

[1] *Apology* 61:12.

already appeared in Colossians (3:16), but the presence here of a part of a Christian hymn shows unmistakably that such a literature is now definitely developing. The earliest hymns of the Church were of course Jewish psalms, like those sung at the Last Supper. Extempore religious singing too seems to have been among the practices of the Corinthian church. But Luke-Acts clearly shows that a definite Christian hymnology was developing—The Lucan canticles—and the choruses and antiphonies of the Revelation confirm this impression. Here belongs this baptismal fragment in Ephesians, a fresh and very concrete illustration of what Walter Pater called the Church's "wholly unparalleled genius for liturgy." Already "she was rapidly reorganizing pagan and Jewish elements of ritual for the expanding therein of her own heart of devotion."[2] It is true Pater says this of the days of the Antonines, but the process was already under way, in the Canticles of Luke and in the choruses, arias, and antiphonies of the Revelation.

[2] *Marius the Epicurean*, p. 277.

XI
5:22–33

You married women must subordinate yourselves to your husbands, as you do to the Lord, for a husband is the head of his wife, just as Christ is the head of the church, which is his body, and is saved by him. Just as the church is in subjection to Christ, so married women must be, in everything, to their husbands. You who are husbands must love your wives, just as Christ loves the church and gave himself for her, to consecrate her, after cleansing her with the bath in water through her confession of him, in order to bring the church to himself in all her beauty, without a flaw or a wrinkle or anything of the kind, but to be consecrated and faultless. That is the way husbands ought to love their wives—as if they were their own bodies; a man who loves his wife is really loving himself, for no one ever hates his own person, but he feeds it and takes care of it, just as Christ does with the church, for we are parts of his body. Therefore a man must leave his father and mother and attach himself to his wife, and they must become one. This is a great secret, but I understand it of Christ and the church. But each one of you must love his wife just as he loves himself, and the wife, too, must respect her husband.

Marriage Symbolizes Christ's Union With The Church

Following a plan already before him in Colossians (3:18—4:1), the writer describes the special duties of wives, husbands, children, fathers, slaves, and masters (5:22—6:9). The chief interest here attaches to his peculiar development of what was there so summary and concise, and his expansions prove to be exceedingly significant.

To the relation of husbands and wives, which Colossians dismissed with two or three lines, our writer devotes twenty (5:22-33), not so much because of his interest in the marriage relation as because he sees in it a glorious parable of the mystic union between Christ and the Church—of course the Church Universal, of which he has already said so much. As we read the paragraph (5:22-33) we come to perceive that the writer is not so much exalting the marriage relation by comparing it to the union of Christ and the Church, as illuminating and adorning that doctrine by entwining it with the most familiar, intimate, and fruitful of human relations. The germ of this he found, of course, in Paul, but its full development was to come very shortly after, in the glorious picture of the Revelation (chap. 21). The Church must be obedient to Christ, confess him, and accept baptism and consecration, so as attain the purity and beauty the relation implies. Christ too loves and cares for the Church, with which he is thus mystically united. Here is the great allegory, the marriage of Christ and the Church. The high duty and destiny of the Church, and the necessity that it be kept pure and unified in life and doctrine, and intimately united with the mind of Christ, are powerfully combined in the figure. Of course a lofty conception of the husband's part is also involved in it; he must love his wife, and the wife too must respect her husband; but the impression remains that it is the symbol much more than the substance that attracts and absorbs the writer.

XII
6:1–4

Children, as Christians obey your parents, for that is right. "You must honor your father and mother"—that is the first commandment accompanied with a promise—"so that you may prosper and have a long life on earth." You fathers, too, must not irritate your children, but you must bring them up with Christian training and instruction.

Children and Parents

The paragraph on the duties of children and parents, 6:1–4, is in its own way quite as striking as that on wives and husbands. The suggestion for it is of course found in three lines of Colossians, 3:20, 21, which have been expanded in Ephesians to six, with the aid of the fifth commandment, Exod. 20:12. But the striking change comes in the admonition to fathers to bring their children up with Christian training and instruction. Colossians was content with an amazingly limited description of the duty of the Christian father: "Do not irritate your children, or they may lose heart." Paul's own picture of his paternal attitude to the Thessalonians goes much beyond it: "You know how, like a father with his children, we used to urge, encourage and implore you to make your lives worthy of God, ..." but of course the Thessalonians were not really children, but grown people. In Ephesians, too, fathers are told not to irritate their children, with this striking addition however: "You must bring them up with Christian training and instruction."

The indifference with which this passage is treated by those who accept the Pauline authorship of Ephesians is a striking indictment of their general position. To them it appears simply an obvious commonplace. How entirely out of place it would be in the mouth of Paul escapes them. With his expectation of the early end of the world Paul had no thought for the training of children. It has often been pointed out that they seemed to him the symbol of immaturity and imperfection. He perceives, however, that fathers must not needlessly irritate and discourage them. To us it seems almost incredible that he should not go beyond this; and one might affirm that these verses in Ephesians show an advance in his thinking upon what he so meagerly says in Col. 3:21. But this fits very badly with the idea that the two letters were written and sent at the same time, if they are both by Paul.

It must be clear that a man who could ever have treated the duties of fatherhood so barrenly as the author of Col. 3:21 could never have written Eph. 6:4. A world of Christian reflection and experience lies between these two statements. We cannot agree with Scott that "the verse can hardly be construed as a warning to Christian parents to instruct their children in the facts and principles of their religion." The children have already been told to adopt a Christian attitude toward their parents (6:1), and we can hardly suppose that they learned this in Sunday school. They learned it from their parents, and their parents must impart it to them.

The passage, short and simple as it seems, points to a time when it begins to be seen that the future of the Church depends in no small measure on its children, and its first duty is to them. Already in Luke-Acts there is a dawning interest in education, and it is not too much to say that in this commonplace verse in Ephesians we have the first sign of Christian education in the home, which was to mean so much in men like Origen and Augustine and millions of others, from then till now. But it unmistakably reflects an age when Paul's vivid and immediate apocalyptic expectation had waned, and if the verses about the Church as the bride of Christ suggest the age of the Revelation, this verse shows we are well on our way toward the age and interests of the Pastorals.

XIII
6:5–9

You who are slaves, obey your earthly masters, in reverence and awe, with sincerity of heart, as you would the Christ, not with mere external service, as though you had only men to please, but like slaves of Christ, carrying out the will of God. Do your duties heartily and willingly, as though it were for the Lord, not for men, for you know that everyone, slave or free, will be rewarded by the Lord for his good conduct. You who are masters, too, must treat your slaves in the same way, and cease to threaten them, for you know that their Master and yours is in heaven, and that he will show no partiality.

Slaves and Masters

The special injunctions to slaves and masters follow pretty closely the sentences on the same subject in Colossians, 3:22—4:1. The thought that everyone, whether slave or free, will be rewarded by the Lord for his good conduct (vs. 8) has a somewhat leveling sound, absent from the Colossians passage; and the command to masters to cease to threaten their slaves (vs. 9) suggests a broader and more concrete acquaintance with the actual workings of ancient slavery than Colossians.[1] One is reminded of the slave Epictetus whose leg was broken by his master. The suggestion of reciprocity, "You masters must treat your slaves in the same way" (vs. 9), sounds almost like the Golden Rule, and is so understood by Scott (p. 246).

---

[1] Rylands Papyri (I, 28, l. 117) mentions ἀπειλαὶ καὶ μόχθοι, "threats and hardships," as portended for a slave by certain signs.

XIV
6:10-20

Henceforth you must grow strong through union with the Lord and through his mighty strength. You must put on God's armor, so as to be able to stand up against the devil's stratagems. For we have to struggle, not with enemies of flesh and blood, but with the hierarchies, the authorities, the master-spirits of this dark world, the spirit-forces of evil on high. So you must take God's armor, so that when the evil day comes you will be able to make a stand, and when it is all over to hold your ground. Stand your ground, then, with the belt of truth around your waist, and put on uprightness as your coat of mail, and on your feet put the readiness the good news of peace brings. Besides all these, take faith for your shield, for with it you will be able to put out all the flaming missiles of the evil one, and take salvation for your helmet, and for your sword the Spirit, which is the voice of God. Use every kind of prayer and entreaty, and at every opportunity pray in the Spirit. Be on the alert about it; devote yourselves constantly to prayer for all God's people and for me, that when I open my lips I may be given a message, so that I may boldly make known the secret of the good news, for the sake of which I am an envoy, and in prison. Pray that, when I tell it, I may have the courage to speak as I ought.

The Christian Warfare and Armor

The specific duties of various groups in the Church are followed by a description of the Christian warfare which all must take part in (6:10-20). The Christian is the soldier of Christ. His enemy is the devil, and all the spiritual forces of evil under his command. What armor one needs for such a war! When that trying day comes, the Christian must hold his ground, with the belt of truth about his waist, with uprightness for his coat-of-mail, with the readiness of the gospel of peace upon his feet; with the shield of faith, the helmet of salvation, and the sword of the Spirit, which is the voice of God. Prayer is to be a constant attitude and exercise, not simply a matter of public worship or of morning or evening routine. It is not to be droned over with absent mind, but to be gone about with wide-awake earnestness, on behalf of all Christians, and for Paul himself and his presentation of the gospel. This prayer by all Christians, for all Christians, fits extremely well with the encyclical character of the epistle and would tend strongly to the sense of solidarity so important to the unity of the Church Universal.

Everyone is struck with the completeness of the divine armor as described here. It is gathered from the armories of Isaiah (chaps. 11, 52, 59), Wisdom (5:17-20), Luke (11:22), and I Thessalonians, into a completer picture than any of those books affords. The suggestions of I Thessalonians seem to have been built up with the aid of these other military allusions, with just that literary care and skill that Paul so expressly avoided and disavowed in I Corinthians.

And how short a step it is from this account of the weapons of the Christian warfare to the "good soldier of Christ Jesus," in II Tim. 2:4. Here again Ephesians is halfway from Paul to the Pastoral letters.

The devil (vs. 11), as we have seen, is a word for Satan not found in Paul's letters; Ephesians uses it here and in 4:27 above.

Verse 18 strongly suggests a time when prayer had begun to be formal and a matter of routine. That this soon came to be the case is shown from the Teaching of the Twelve Apostles, in its Greek form reflecting the developments of the first half of the second century, which enjoins the offering of the Lord's Prayer three times a day. Set prayers and hours of prayer were part of the Christian inheritance from Judaism, so that a formal conception of prayer was present in the Church from the beginning, side by side with the freer ways of prayer so often reflected in Paul. Regular and formal prayer seems now to be threatening the free expression of the impulses of the Spirit. The writer of Ephesians would correct this, without sacrificing the values of the other type: "Use every kind of prayer and entreaty, and at every opportunity pray in the Spirit. Be on the alert about it. Devote yourselves constantly to prayer. . . . ." The influence of Luke 21:36 seems unmistakable here: the combination "Be vigilant . . . . on every occasion . . . . praying," ἀγρυπνεῖτε δὲ ἐν παντὶ καιρῷ δεόμενοι, can hardly be a mere coincidence.

"I am an envoy, and in prison" (vs. 19) reminds us of II Cor. 5:20, "It is for Christ . . . . that I am an envoy." Acts 28:20 uses the word "chain," τὴν ἅλυσιν ταύτην περίκειμαι, which is used here, ἐν ἁλύσει. But the combination of the idea of embassy with imprisonment is derived from Philemon, "no less an envoy of Christ Jesus, though now a prisoner for him," πρεσβύτης νυνὶ δὲ καὶ δέσμιος. We have already noted the influence of Philemon upon Eph. 3:1, (ὁ) δέσμιος (τοῦ) Χριστοῦ Ἰησοῦ. The writer of Ephesians clearly understood the much-discussed πρεσβύτης not in the sense of "old man," but as Lightfoot long ago perceived it should be understood, of "envoy." The difference in spelling is really immaterial, as II Macc. 11:34, πρεσβῦται Ῥωμαίων, "ambassadors of the Romans," shows. In Ephesians we see how the word was understood by the earliest interpreters of Philemon. The word is of great importance for the whole tone of Philemon. Taken in the sense of "old man," it leaves the impression of the letter weak, sentimental, and pathetic, while the sense of ambassador reveals it as strong, authoritative, indomitable. It is not too much to say that it is the key to Philemon. Thus Ephesians historically approached throws important light upon the early understanding of Philemon.

XV
6:21-24

In order that you also may know how I am, our dear brother Tychicus, a faithful helper in the Lord's service, will tell you all about it. That is the very reason I am sending him, to let you know how I am, and to cheer your hearts.

Farewell

God our Father and the Lord Jesus Christ give the brothers peace and love, with faith. God's blessing be with all who have an unfailing love for our Lord Jesus Christ.

The close of the epistle, like the beginning, conforms to the Pauline disguise in which it is cast; Tychicus, the messenger to Colossae and Philemon, appears as the bearer of this prison encyclical, though how he could have carried it to all the Christians of the day is of course perplexing. But no more so than how Paul himself could have come to write an encyclical letter to Christendom. Tychicus is just such a problem as "Mark my son," in I Pet. 5:13, and "our brother Timothy," in Heb. 13:23. He is part of the pseudepigraphical guise of the epistle, which here leans heavily upon Colossians.

In the closing benedictions, an un-Pauline and clearly encyclical touch appears. Both are in the third person: "God our Father and the Lord Jesus Christ give the brothers peace and love with faith. God's blessing be with all who have an unfailing love for our Lord Jesus Christ." In the letters of Paul, the closing blessings are always directly "upon you," "to you." One feels that the Pauline forms have been built up and generalized, peace, love, faith, blessing being combined, instead of the simpler Pauline

"Blessing" or "Blessing, love." The fuller one at the end of II Corinthians probably marked the close of the Pauline corpus, in its earliest form.

On the whole, then, the objective and encyclical character of the benedictions is clear; the writer's prayer is that the great typical Christian blessings—peace, love, faith, and the favor of God—may rest upon all the brotherhood everywhere. The use of "the brothers" for the whole Christian fellowship, which is proved by the parallel expression "all who love," in the next verse, is not found in Paul, and is very close to "the brotherhood" in I Pet. 2:17, 5:9, in the same wide sense of the whole Christian fellowship. The epistle thus closes with the same encyclical note that was struck at its beginning.

CONCLUSION

It seems abundantly clear that the epistle is full of matters that have to be suppressed or ignored if it is to be interpreted as a work of Paul himself, or even a Paulinist writing before the Pauline letters had been collected; but which blossom into full significance if the epistle be understood as an introduction to the Pauline letters, when first they were offered to the churches, by the hand that had patiently gathered them from the obscurity into which they had naturally fallen. The epistle thus opens its full meaning only to this approach, and the charges of vagueness, wordiness, vanity, and failure to reflect definite conditions fall to the ground. The test to which we have subjected the theory advanced as to the origin of the epistle is fully met; the theory illumines the whole letter, and offers a definite situation for its composition which throws a convincing light upon page after page. The perplexities of the Pauline interpreters evaporate in the presence of a sound understanding of the historical occasion which led to the writing of the epistle. The critical facts established by a long series of able students of the epistle have been frankly accepted and built upon. They should, if they are sound, be viewed not as difficulties to be explained away; but clues, of the utmost value, to be closely followed. We have sought to follow out these clues, being convinced that the truth will lead us farther than any merely traditional views about Ephesians, no matter how prized or established they may be. The result has justified our hopes. The epistle does yield its meaning more fully and naturally than on other theories of its origin. At every point it is seen to fit definitely into situations we know to have existed toward the end of the first century.

Certain fugitive suggestions that have been offered as to the relation of Ephesians to the Pauline corpus are thus seen to be well grounded and to fit admirably together. Holtzmann's elaborate studies of the problem of Ephesians-Colossians saw in the writer of Ephesians a man interested in the collection of the Pauline remains, possessed of a considerable number of Pauline letters, and concerned in revising at least two of them, Romans and Colossians.

Juelicher a generation later felt that on most accounts the natural explanation of the purpose and aim of Ephesians was that it was to serve as introduction to a collection of Pauline letters; and more recently Johannes Weiss declared it not yet settled whether the author of Ephesians was not the actual collector of the Pauline corpus.

Juelicher once said that no one had produced a clear picture of the situation in which a *Paulus redivivus* might have composed Ephesians. We venture to accept this very proper challenge with the hypothesis that the publication of Luke-Acts early in the nineties led an Asian Christian, perhaps from Colossae, and at any rate already acquainted with Colossians-Philemon, to search among the Pauline churches revealed in Acts for other literary remains of Paul; that what he found in the course of a few months or years so stirred him that he published it among the churches, introducing the collection to his Christian contemporaries with the letter we know as Ephesians, in which he sought to awaken the churches from lethargy and formalism, to unite them against the sects, and to acquaint them with the great religious values to be found in the collected letters of Paul, then assembled and published for the first time. To this position the critical facts and literary considerations definitely point, and with it the interpretation of the letter surprisingly accords.

PART II
EPHESIANS AND THE PAULINE LETTERS

EPHESIANS AND THE PAULINE LETTERS

The relation of Ephesians to the nine letters usually recognized as genuine writings of Paul is so extraordinary and so significant as to call for detailed exhibition in tabular form. Hardly a line of Ephesians is unaffected by those letters, in ideas if not in language, and every one of those letters has made some contribution to Ephesians. This cannot be accident. Even when the writer has ideas of his own to express he does so as far as possible in Pauline forms of speech. We cannot imagine Paul himself as being so entirely limited by what he had previously written, still less by just those of his writings that eventually survived. We have seen that in every letter of his he uncovers some new area of thought. Testing a random passage in Paul (Phil., chap. 2) in the same way, my friends Mr. James R. Branton and Mr. George F. Hall have found that the utmost that can be satisfied in that chapter from the other letters is 45 per cent, and only 20 per cent is really convincing. But in Ephesians fully 88 per cent is convincingly paralleled in the other letters.[1]

The writer must have been definitely holding himself to the materials supplied by the nine letters, to have produced this result. The bearing of this fact upon the problem of Ephesians has not, it would seem, been fully recognized or taken account of, for its significance for the origin of the letter is decisive. In what circumstances, we are compelled

[1] Of the remainder, one-fourth, or 3 per cent of the total, is Old Testament quotations or reminiscences.

to ask, could such a thing have taken place? I cannot find that this question has been raised, still less answered, by writers on New Testament introduction or by interpreters of the letter.

I can imagine no more natural and probable explanation than that the writer of Ephesians has found and assembled the Pauline letters, and, profoundly moved by their religious value, has undertaken to introduce them to the Christian world, prefacing them with a letter cast in Pauline forms and bearing the name of Paul, but seeking to bridge the generation that has elapsed since Paul's death, and bring his message to bear more directly upon the needs of the writer's day, when sectarianism and apathy were undermining the churches. This would explain, as nothing else will, the writer's sedulous holding to what Paul had previously said, in just those nine letters of his which have come down to us.

This exhibit is also fatal to the current notion that the Pauline letters leaked gradually into circulation, for, if so, how could the first work to reflect any of them reflect them all? Every one of the nine letters, even II Thessalonians and Philemon, is convincingly reflected in Ephesians.

I earnestly hope that students and scholars who are skeptical about these claims will take the trouble to examine this exhibit in detail, for only so can they form a sound impression as to the seriousness of the problem and the soundness of the solution for it that I have ventured to advance.

I do not present even this exhibit as an exhaustive showing of the use made in Ephesians of the nine genuine letters of Paul; the task may be still more thoroughly done. What I have sought to do is only to carry it to the point of demonstration; anything more than that could hardly be important or affect the conclusions established by the exhibit.

In preparing this conspectus I have been helped by the work of my friend Professor Albert E. Barnett, of Scarritt College, Nashville, Tennessee, and have taken advantage of the studies of earlier workers, notably Holtzmann and von Soden.[2]

The first column presents the continuous text of Ephesians broken into short lines to show its resemblances to the text of Colossians or the other letters of Paul. The parallel parts of Colossians are shown in the second column, and those of the other Pauline letters in columns 3 and 4. The lower margin contains parallels from the Septuagint Old Testament and from Luke-Acts, together with a few additional parallels from Colossians and the other Pauline letters for which there was not room in columns 2, 3, and 4.

The text printed below is that of Westcott and Hort, and is used with the very kind permission of Messrs. Macmillan and Company, Ltd., the holders of the copyright. We have omitted only their marginal readings and their half-brackets. Quotation marks inclose words printed by them in uncials.

[2] Holtzmann, *Kritik der Epheser- und Kolosserbriefe;* von Soden, "Der Epheserbrief," *Jahrbücher für die protestantische Theologie*, XIII (1887), 103 ff.

EPHESIANS	COLOSSIAN PARALLELS
1	1:1, 2
1 ΠΑΥΛΟΣ ἀπόστολος Χριστοῦ Ἰησοῦ διὰ θελήματος θεοῦ τοῖς ἁγίοις τοῖς οὖσιν [[ἐν Ἐφέσῳ]] καὶ πιστοῖς ἐν Χριστῷ Ἰησοῦ·[1]	ΠΑΥΛΟΣ ἀπόστολος Χριστοῦ Ἰησοῦ διὰ θελήματος θεοῦ .... τοῖς ἐν Κολοσσαῖς ἁγίοις καὶ πιστοῖς ἀδελφοῖς ἐν Χριστῷ·
2 χάρις ὑμῖν καὶ εἰρήνη ἀπὸ θεοῦ πατρὸς ἡμῶν καὶ κυρίου Ἰησοῦ Χριστοῦ.	χάρις ὑμῖν καὶ εἰρήνη ἀπὸ θεοῦ πατρὸς ἡμῶν.
3 Εὐλογητὸς ὁ θεὸς καὶ πατὴρ τοῦ κυρίου ἡμῶν Ἰησοῦ Χριστοῦ, ὁ εὐλογήσας ἡμᾶς ἐν πάσῃ εὐλογίᾳ πνευματικῇ ἐν τοῖς ἐπουρανίοις ἐν Χριστῷ,	
	3:12b
4 καθὼς ἐξελέξατο ἡμᾶς ἐν αὐτῷ[2]	ὡς ἐκλεκτοὶ τοῦ θεοῦ,
πρὸ καταβολῆς κόσμου,[3]	
	1:22b
εἶναι ἡμᾶς ἁγίους καὶ ἀμώμους	παραστῆσαι ὑμᾶς ἁγίους καὶ ἀμώμους
κατενώπιον αὐτοῦ ἐν ἀγάπῃ,	καὶ ἀνεγκλήτους κατενώπιον αὐτοῦ,
5 προορίσας ἡμᾶς εἰς υἱοθεσίαν	

[3] Rev. 13:8b, 17:8b, ἀπὸ καταβολῆς κόσμου.

[1] 1:4a, ἐν Χριστῷ Ἰησοῦ.

Other Pauline Parallels

II Cor. 1:1–3
ΠΑΥΛΟΣ ἀπόστολος Χριστοῦ Ἰησοῦ
διὰ θελήματος θεοῦ ....
σὺν τοῖς ἁγίοις πᾶσιν τοῖς οὖσιν
ἐν ὅλῃ τῇ Ἀχαίᾳ·

χάρις ὑμῖν καὶ εἰρήνη
ἀπὸ θεοῦ πατρὸς ἡμῶν
καὶ κυρίου Ἰησοῦ Χριστοῦ.
Εὐλογητὸς ὁ θεὸς καὶ πατὴρ
τοῦ κυρίου ἡμῶν Ἰησοῦ Χριστοῦ,
ὁ πατὴρ τῶν οἰκτιρμῶν

καὶ θεὸς πάσης παρακλήσεως,

Gal. 3:14a
ἵνα εἰς τὰ ἔθνη ἡ εὐλογία τοῦ Ἀβραὰμ
γένηται ἐν Ἰησοῦ Χριστῷ,
Rom. 1:11a
ἵνα τι μεταδῶ χάρισμα ὑμῖν πνευματικὸν

Cf. ἐπουράνιος Phil. 2:10; I Cor. 15:40–49

II Thess. 2:13b
ὅτι εἵλατο ὑμᾶς ὁ θεὸς

I Cor. 1:27a
ἀλλὰ τὰ μωρὰ τοῦ κόσμου ἐξελέξατο ὁ θεός,

I Cor. 2:7b
ἣν προώρισεν ὁ θεὸς πρὸ τῶν αἰώνων εἰς δόξαν ἡμῶν·

ἀπ' ἀρχῆς

II Thess. 2:13b
εἰς σωτηρίαν ἐν ἁγιασμῷ πνεύματος
Cf. Rom. 5:1–11
Rom. 8:29
ὅτι οὓς προέγνω, καὶ προώρισεν συμμόρφους τῆς εἰκόνος τοῦ υἱοῦ αὐτοῦ, εἰς τὸ εἶναι αὐτὸν πρωτότοκον ἐν πολλοῖς ἀδελφοῖς·

Gal. 4:5b
ἵνα τὴν υἱοθεσίαν ἀπολάβωμεν.

Gal. 3:26
Πάντες γὰρ υἱοὶ θεοῦ ἐστε

Cf. 8:15, 23

---

[2] I Cor. 1:6, καθὼς τὸ μαρτύριον τοῦ χριστοῦ ἐβεβαιώθη ἐν ὑμῖν.

EPHESIANS 1	COLOSSIAN PARALLELS
διὰ Ἰησοῦ Χριστοῦ εἰς αὐτόν,	
6 κατὰ τὴν εὐδοκίαν τοῦ θελήματος αὐτοῦ,	
εἰς ἔπαινον δόξης τῆς χάριτος αὐτοῦ	
	1:13b, 14a
ἧς ἐχαρίτωσεν ἡμᾶς ἐν τῷ ἠγαπημένῳ,	τοῦ υἱοῦ τῆς ἀγάπης αὐτοῦ,
7 ἐν ᾧ ἔχομεν τὴν ἀπολύτρωσιν	ἐν ᾧ ἔχομεν τὴν ἀπολύτρωσιν,
	1:20b
διὰ τοῦ αἵματος αὐτοῦ,	εἰρηνοποιήσας διὰ τοῦ αἵματος τοῦ σταυροῦ αὐτοῦ,
	1:14b
τὴν ἄφεσιν τῶν παραπτωμάτων,	τὴν ἄφεσιν τῶν ἁμαρτιῶν·
8 κατὰ τὸ πλοῦτος τῆς χάριτος αὐτοῦ	
	1:9b
ἧς ἐπερίσσευσεν εἰς ἡμᾶς	ἵνα πληρωθῆτε τὴν ἐπίγνωσιν τοῦ θελήματος αὐτοῦ
9 ἐν πάσῃ σοφίᾳ καὶ φρονήσει	ἐν πάσῃ σοφίᾳ καὶ συνέσει πνευματικῇ,
	1:27a
γνωρίσας ἡμῖν	οἷς ἠθέλησεν ὁ θεὸς γνωρίσαι τί τὸ πλοῦτος
τὸ μυστήριον τοῦ θελήματος αὐτοῦ,	τῆς δόξης τοῦ μυστηρίου τούτου ἐν τοῖς ἔθνεσιν,

Other Pauline Parallels

See Phil. 1:11*b* below

Phil. 2:13

θεὸς γάρ ἐστιν ὁ ἐνεργῶν ἐν ὑμῖν καὶ τὸ θέλειν καὶ τὸ ἐνεργεῖν ὑπὲρ τῆς εὐδοκίας·

Phil. 1:11*b*

τὸν διὰ Ἰησοῦ Χριστοῦ εἰς δόξαν καὶ ἔπαινον θεοῦ.

Rom. 5:15*b*

καὶ ἡ δωρεὰ ἐν χάριτι τῇ τοῦ ἑνὸς ἀνθρώπου Ἰησοῦ Χριστοῦ

Rom. 5:9*b*

δικαιωθέντες νῦν ἐν τῷ αἵματι αὐτοῦ

II Cor. 5:19*b*

μὴ λογιζόμενος αὐτοῖς τὰ παραπτώματα αὐτῶν,

Rom. 2:4*a*

ἢ τοῦ πλούτου τῆς χρηστότητος αὐτοῦ

Rom. 11:33*a*

Ὦ βάθος πλούτου

καὶ σοφίας καὶ γνώσεως θεοῦ·

I Cor. 2:7*a*

ἀλλὰ λαλοῦμεν

θεοῦ σοφίαν ἐν μυστηρίῳ....
ἣν προώρισεν

διὰ τῆς πίστεως ἐν Χριστῷ Ἰησοῦ.

Cf. Rom. 5:1-11

II Cor. 9:14*b*, 15

διὰ τὴν ὑπερβάλλουσαν χάριν τοῦ θεοῦ ἐφ᾽ ὑμῖν.

Χάρις τῷ θεῷ ἐπὶ τῇ ἀνεκδιηγήτῳ αὐτοῦ δωρεᾷ.

Rom. 3:25, 26*a*

ὃν προέθετο ὁ θεὸς ἱλαστήριον

διὰ πίστεως ἐν τῷ αὐτοῦ αἵματι εἰς ἔνδειξιν τῆς δικαιοσύνης αὐτοῦ

διὰ τὴν πάρεσιν τῶν προγεγονότων ἁμαρτημάτων
ἐν τῇ ἀνοχῇ τοῦ θεοῦ,

Rom. 5:15*b*

ἡ χάρις τοῦ θεοῦ καὶ ἡ δωρεὰ ἐν χάριτι τῇ τοῦ ἑνὸς ἀνθρώπου Ἰησοῦ Χριστοῦ

εἰς τοὺς πολλοὺς ἐπερίσσευσεν.

Rom. 16:25*b*, 26*a*

κατὰ ἀποκάλυψιν (see below)

μυστηρίου χρόνοις αἰωνίοις σεσιγημένου
φανερωθέντος δὲ νῦν διά τε γραφῶν προφητικῶν

EPHESIANS 1	COLOSSIAN PARALLELS
κατὰ τὴν εὐδοκίαν αὐτοῦ	
ἣν προέθετο ἐν αὐτῷ⁴	
	1:25b; cf. 26
10 εἰς οἰκονομίαν τοῦ πληρώματος τῶν καιρῶν,	κατὰ τὴν οἰκονομίαν . . . . πληρῶσαι τὸν λόγον
	1:20; cf. 1:18; 2:10
ἀνακεφαλαιώσασθαι τὰ πάντα ἐν τῷ χριστῷ,	καὶ δι' αὐτοῦ ἀποκαταλλάξαι τὰ πάντα εἰς αὐτόν, ...
τὰ ἐπὶ τοῖς οὐρανοῖς καὶ τὰ ἐπὶ τῆς γῆς·	εἴτε τὰ ἐπὶ τῆς γῆς εἴτε τὰ ἐν τοῖς οὐρανοῖς·
	Cf. 1:16a
	1:12b
11 ἐν αὐτῷ, ἐν ᾧ καὶ ἐκληρώθημεν	τῷ ἱκανώσαντι ὑμᾶς εἰς τὴν μερίδα τοῦ κλήρου τῶν ἁγίων ἐν τῷ φωτί,
προορισθέντες κατὰ πρόθεσιν	
τοῦ τὰ πάντα ἐνεργοῦντος	
κατὰ τὴν βουλὴν τοῦ θελήματος αὐτοῦ,	
12 εἰς τὸ εἶναι ἡμᾶς	
εἰς ἔπαινον δόξης αὐτοῦ	
τοὺς προηλπικότας ἐν τῷ χριστῷ·	

Other Pauline Parallels

Rom. 8:28b; cf. 9:11
τοῖς κατὰ (cf. Phil. 2:13b above)
πρόθεσιν κλητοῖς οὖσιν.

Gal. 4:4a
ὅτε δὲ ἦλθεν τὸ πλήρωμα τοῦ χρόνου,

Rom. 13:9b
ἐν τῷ λόγῳ τούτῳ ἀνακεφαλαιοῦται,

κατ' ἐπιταγὴν τοῦ αἰωνίου θεοῦ
εἰς ὑπακοὴν πίστεως
εἰς πάντα τὰ ἔθνη γνωρισθέντος,

Cf. I Cor. 10:11b
εἰς οὓς τὰ τέλη τῶν αἰώνων κατήντηκεν.

Cf. I Cor. 15:27

Rom. 8:28b–30a
πάντα συνεργεῖ [ὁ θεὸς] εἰς ἀγαθόν,
τοῖς κατὰ πρόθεσιν κλητοῖς οὖσιν.
ὅτι οὓς προέγνω, καὶ προώρισεν
. . . . οὓς δὲ προώρισεν, τούτους καὶ ἐκάλεσεν·

I Cor. 12:6b
ὁ ἐνεργῶν τὰ πάντα ἐν πᾶσιν.

Rom. 9:19b
τῷ γὰρ βουλήματι αὐτοῦ τίς ἀνθέστηκεν;

Rom. 9:23, 24
ἵνα γνωρίσῃ
τὸν πλοῦτον τῆς δόξης αὐτοῦ ἐπὶ σκεύη ἐλέους,
ἃ προητοίμασεν εἰς δόξαν, οὓς καὶ ἐκάλεσεν ἡμᾶς οὐ μόνον ἐξ Ἰουδαίων

Rom. 9:11b
ἵνα ἡ κατ' ἐκλογὴν πρόθεσις τοῦ θεοῦ μένῃ,

Phil. 2:13
θεὸς γάρ ἐστιν ὁ ἐνεργῶν ἐν ὑμῖν καὶ τὸ θέλειν καὶ τὸ ἐνεργεῖν ὑπὲρ τῆς εὐδοκίας·

Gal. 1:4b
κατὰ τὸ θέλημα τοῦ θεοῦ καὶ πατρὸς ἡμῶν

Phil. 1:11b
εἰς δόξαν καὶ ἔπαινον θεοῦ.

Rom. 8:30c
τούτους καὶ ἐδόξασεν.

[4] Rom. 3:25a, ὃν προέθετο ὁ θεὸς ἱλαστήριον.

EPHESIANS 1	Colossian Parallels
	1:5b
13 ἐν ᾧ καὶ ὑμεῖς ἀκούσαντες	ἧν προηκούσατε
τὸν λόγον τῆς ἀληθείας,	ἐν τῷ λόγῳ τῆς ἀληθείας
τὸ εὐαγγέλιον τῆς σωτηρίας ὑμῶν,	τοῦ εὐαγγελίου τοῦ παρόντος εἰς ὑμᾶς,
ἐν ᾧ καὶ πιστεύσαντες ἐσφραγίσθητε[5] τῷ πνεύματι τῆς ἐπαγγελίας τῷ ἁγίῳ,	
	1:12b
14 ὅ ἐστιν ἀρραβὼν τῆς κληρονομίας ἡμῶν,	εἰς τὴν μερίδα τοῦ κλήρου τῶν ἁγίων
	1:14a
εἰς ἀπολύτρωσιν τῆς περιποιήσεως,	ἐν ᾧ ἔχομεν τὴν ἀπολύτρωσιν,
εἰς ἔπαινον τῆς δόξης αὐτοῦ.	1:9a
15 Διὰ τοῦτο κἀγώ,	Διὰ τοῦτο καὶ ἡμεῖς, ἀφ' ἧς ἡμέρας ἠκούσαμεν,
	1:4
ἀκούσας τὴν καθ' ὑμᾶς πίστιν	ἀκούσαντες τὴν πίστιν ὑμῶν
ἐν τῷ κυρίῳ Ἰησοῦ καὶ τὴν εἰς πάντας τοὺς ἁγίους,	ἐν Χριστῷ Ἰησοῦ καὶ τὴν ἀγάπην [ἣν ἔχετε] εἰς πάντας τοὺς ἁγίους
	1:9b
16 οὐ παύομαι[6]	οὐ παυόμεθα ὑπὲρ ὑμῶν προσευχόμενοι καὶ αἰτούμενοι

Other Pauline Parallels

ἀλλὰ καὶ ἐξ ἐθνῶν—;
  II Cor. 6:7
ἐν λόγῳ ἀληθείας,
  Rom. 1:16b
τὸ εὐαγγέλιον, δύναμις γὰρ θεοῦ ἐστὶν εἰς σωτηρίαν
  II Cor. 1:22; cf. 5:5
[ὁ] καὶ σφραγισάμενος ἡμᾶς

καὶ δοὺς τὸν ἀρραβῶνα

τοῦ πνεύματος ἐν ταῖς καρδίαις ἡμῶν.
  Rom. 8:23b; cf. 3:24b
υἱοθεσίαν ἀπεκδεχόμενοι
τὴν ἀπολύτρωσιν τοῦ σώματος ἡμῶν.
  Rom. 1:8
Πρῶτον μὲν εὐχαριστῶ τῷ θεῷ μου διὰ Ἰησοῦ Χριστοῦ περὶ πάντων ὑμῶν,
ὅτι ἡ πίστις ὑμῶν καταγγέλλεται ἐν ὅλῳ τῷ κόσμῳ.

  Rom. 10:14b
πῶς δὲ πιστεύσωσιν οὗ οὐκ ἤκουσαν;

  Gal. 3:14b
ἵνα τὴν ἐπαγγελίαν τοῦ πνεύματος
λάβωμεν διὰ τῆς πίστεως.
  Rom. 8:16, 17a
αὐτὸ τὸ πνεῦμα συμμαρτυρεῖ τῷ πνεύματι ἡμῶν
ὅτι ἐσμὲν τέκνα θεοῦ. εἰ δὲ τέκνα,
καὶ κληρονόμοι·
  I Thess. 5:9b; cf. II Thess. 2:14b
εἰς περιποίησιν σωτηρίας
  Phil. 1:11b
εἰς δόξαν καὶ ἔπαινον θεοῦ.

  Philem. 5
ἀκούων σου τὴν ἀγάπην καὶ τὴν πίστιν ἣν ἔχεις
εἰς τὸν κύριον Ἰησοῦν
καὶ εἰς πάντας τοὺς ἁγίους,

---

[5] Gal. 3:2b, ἐξ ἔργων νόμου τὸ πνεῦμα ἐλάβετε ἢ ἐξ ἀκοῆς πίστεως;

[6] Rom. 1:10a, ὡς ἀδιαλείπτως μνείαν ὑμῶν ποιοῦμαι πάντοτε ἐπὶ τῶν προσευχῶν μου.

EPHESIANS 1	Colossian Parallels
	1:3
εὐχαριστῶν	Εὐχαριστοῦμεν τῷ θεῷ πατρὶ
ὑπὲρ ὑμῶν	See above
	τοῦ κυρίου ἡμῶν Ἰησοῦ [Χριστοῦ]
μνείαν ποιούμενος	
ἐπὶ τῶν προσευχῶν μου,	πάντοτε περὶ ὑμῶν προσευχόμενοι,
	1:9c
17 ἵνα ὁ θεὸς τοῦ κυρίου ἡμῶν Ἰησοῦ Χριστοῦ,	ἵνα
ὁ πατὴρ τῆς δόξης,[7]	
δῴη ὑμῖν	πληρωθῆτε
πνεῦμα σοφίας καὶ ἀποκαλύψεως	See below
ἐν ἐπιγνώσει αὐτοῦ,	τὴν ἐπίγνωσιν τοῦ θελήματος αὐτοῦ ἐν πάσῃ σοφίᾳ καὶ συνέσει πνευματικῇ,
	1:12b
18 πεφωτισμένους	εἰς τὴν μερίδα τοῦ κλήρου τῶν ἁγίων ἐν τῷ φωτί,
	1:26b, 27
τοὺς ὀφθαλμοὺς τῆς καρδίας [ὑμῶν]	νῦν δὲ ἐφανερώθη τοῖς ἁγίοις αὐτοῦ,
εἰς τὸ εἰδέναι ὑμᾶς	οἷς ἠθέλησεν ὁ θεὸς γνωρίσαι
τίς ἐστιν ἡ ἐλπὶς τῆς κλήσεως αὐτοῦ,	See below
τίς ὁ πλοῦτος τῆς δόξης	τί τὸ πλοῦτος τῆς δόξης
τῆς "κληρονομίας" αὐτοῦ[8]	τοῦ μυστηρίου τούτου
"ἐν τοῖς ἁγίοις,"[9]	ἐν τοῖς ἔθνεσιν,
	ὅ ἐστιν Χριστὸς ἐν ὑμῖν,
	ἡ ἐλπὶς τῆς δόξης·

[8] Deut. 33:4b, κληρονομίαν συναγωγαῖς Ἰακώβ.

[9] 1:12b, εἰς τὴν μερίδα τοῦ κλήρου τῶν ἁγίων ἐν τῷ φωτί.

Other Pauline Parallels

Phil. 1:3
Εὐχαριστῶ τῷ θεῷ μου

ἐπὶ πάσῃ τῇ μνείᾳ ὑμῶν
πάντοτε ἐν πάσῃ δεήσει μου
ὑπὲρ πάντων ὑμῶν,

II Cor. 11:31a
ὁ θεὸς καὶ πατὴρ τοῦ κυρίου
Ἰησοῦ οἶδεν,

Rom. 6:4b
διὰ τῆς δόξης τοῦ πατρός,

Rom. 5:2b
ἐπ' ἐλπίδι τῆς δόξης τοῦ θεοῦ·

Cf. Rom. 16:25b
κατὰ ἀποκάλυψιν μυστηρίου

Rom. 1:28b
τὸν θεὸν ἔχειν ἐν ἐπιγνώσει,

Cf. II Cor. 4:4b
εἰς τὸ μὴ αὐγάσαι τὸν φωτισμὸν
τοῦ εὐαγγελίου τῆς δόξης τοῦ
χριστοῦ,

Rom. 9:23b
τὸν πλοῦτον τῆς δόξης αὐτοῦ

Philem. 4; cf. I Thess. 1:2; 2:13
Εὐχαριστῶ τῷ θεῷ μου

πάντοτε μνείαν σου ποιούμενος
ἐπὶ τῶν προσευχῶν μου,

Cf. II Cor. 1:3b
ὁ πατὴρ τῶν οἰκτιρμῶν

Cf. Rom. 9:23b
τὸν πλοῦτον τῆς δόξης αὐτοῦ

I Cor. 2:10a; cf. 14:6
ἡμῖν γὰρ ἀπεκάλυψεν ὁ θεὸς διὰ
τοῦ πνεύματος,

Phil. 1:9b
ἐν ἐπιγνώσει καὶ πάσῃ αἰσθήσει,

Cf. Rom. 1:21b; cf. II Cor. 4:6

καὶ ἐσκοτίσθη (cf. I Cor. 4:5)

ἡ ἀσύνετος αὐτῶν καρδία·

---

[7] I Cor. 2:8b, τὸν κύριον τῆς δόξης.

EPHESIANS 1	Colossian Parallels
19 καὶ τί τὸ ὑπερβάλλον μέγεθος	
	1:11a
τῆς δυνάμεως αὐτοῦ	ἐν πάσῃ δυνάμει
εἰς ἡμᾶς τοὺς πιστεύοντας	δυναμούμενοι
κατὰ τὴν ἐνέργειαν τοῦ κράτους[10]	κατὰ τὸ κράτος (cf. 1:29)
τῆς ἰσχύος αὐτοῦ	τῆς δόξης αὐτοῦ
20 ἣν ἐνήργηκεν ἐν τῷ χριστῷ	Cf. 1:29
ἐγείρας αὐτὸν ἐκ νεκρῶν,	See n. 10 below
	3:1b
	τὰ ἄνω ζητεῖτε, οὗ ὁ χριστός ἐστιν
καὶ "καθίσας ἐν δεξιᾷ αὐτοῦ"[11]	"ἐν δεξιᾷ τοῦ θεοῦ καθήμενος·"
ἐν τοῖς ἐπουρανίοις	See above
	2:10b
21 ὑπεράνω πάσης ἀρχῆς καὶ ἐξουσίας	ἡ κεφαλὴ πάσης ἀρχῆς καὶ ἐξουσίας,
	1:16b
καὶ δυνάμεως καὶ κυριότητος	εἴτε θρόνοι εἴτε κυριότητες
	εἴτε ἀρχαὶ εἴτε ἐξουσίαι·
	Cf. 2:15b

[11] Ps. 109 (110):1, Κάθου ἐκ δεξιῶν μου.

[10] 2:12, ἐν ᾧ καὶ συνηγέρθητε διὰ τῆς πίστεως τῆς ἐνεργείας τοῦ θεοῦ τοῦ ἐγείραντος αὐτὸν ἐκ νεκρῶν·

EPHESIANS AND THE PAULINE LETTERS

OTHER PAULINE PARALLELS

II Cor. 9:14b; cf. 3:10
διὰ τὴν ὑπερβάλλουσαν χάριν τοῦ θεοῦ ἐφ' ὑμῖν.

Phil. 3:10b
τὴν δύναμιν τῆς ἀναστάσεως αὐτοῦ

Cf. Rom. 3:22b
εἰς πάντας τοὺς πιστεύοντας,

Phil. 3:21b
κατὰ τὴν ἐνέργειαν τοῦ δύνασθαι αὐτὸν καὶ ὑποτάξαι αὐτῷ τὰ πάντα.

Cf. II Cor. 13:4b
ἐκ δυνάμεως θεοῦ [εἰς ὑμᾶς].
Cf. I Cor. 15:20–28

I Cor. 6:14
ὁ δὲ θεὸς καὶ τὸν κύριον ἤγειρεν καὶ ἡμᾶς ἐξεγερεῖ
διὰ τῆς δυνάμεως αὐτοῦ.

Phil. 2:9, 10
διὸ καὶ ὁ θεὸς αὐτὸν ὑπερύψωσεν,
See below

καὶ ἐχαρίσατο αὐτῷ τὸ ὄνομα τὸ ὑπὲρ

Rom. 8:34
Χριστὸς ['Ιησοῦς] ὁ ἀποθανών,

μᾶλλον δὲ ἐγερθεὶς [ἐκ νεκρῶν],

ὅς ἐστιν "ἐν δεξιᾷ τοῦ θεοῦ,"
Cf. I Cor. 15:40–49

I Cor. 15:24b
ὅταν καταργήσῃ πᾶσαν ἀρχὴν καὶ πᾶσαν ἐξουσίαν

καὶ δύναμιν,

EPHESIANS 1	COLOSSIAN PARALLELS
καὶ παντὸς ὀνόματος ὀνομαζομένου	
οὐ μόνον ἐν τῷ αἰῶνι τούτῳ	
ἀλλὰ καὶ ἐν τῷ μέλλοντι·	
22 καὶ "πάντα ὑπέταξεν ὑπὸ τοὺς πόδας αὐτοῦ," καὶ αὐτὸν ἔδωκεν κεφαλὴν ὑπὲρ πάντα	1:18a καὶ αὐτός ἐστιν ἡ κεφαλὴ
τῇ ἐκκλησίᾳ, 23 ἥτις ἐστὶν τὸ σῶμα αὐτοῦ,[12]	τοῦ σώματος, τῆς ἐκκλησίας· 1:19 ὅτι ἐν αὐτῷ εὐδόκησεν
τὸ πλήρωμα τοῦ τὰ πάντα ἐν πᾶσιν πληρουμένου.[13]	πᾶν τὸ πλήρωμα κατοικῆσαι Cf. 1:16, 17
2 1 καὶ ὑμᾶς ὄντας νεκροὺς τοῖς παραπτώμασιν καὶ ταῖς ἁμαρτίαις ὑμῶν, 2 ἐν αἷς ποτὲ περιεπατήσατε	2:13a καὶ ὑμᾶς νεκροὺς ὄντας τοῖς παραπτώμασιν . . . . ὑμῶν, 3:7a ἐν οἷς καὶ ὑμεῖς περιεπατήσατέ ποτε

[12] Ps. 8:7, πάντα ὑπέταξας ὑποκάτω τῶν ποδῶν αὐτοῦ.

[13] Jer. 23:24b, μὴ οὐχὶ τὸν οὐρανὸν καὶ τὴν γῆν ἐγὼ πληρῶ, λέγει Κύριος;

Other Pauline Parallels

πᾶν ὄνομα, ἵνα ἐν τῷ ὀνόματι Ἰησοῦ "πᾶν γόνυ κάμψῃ" ἐπουρανίων καὶ ἐπιγείων καὶ καταχθονίων,

I Cor. 2:6b (cf. 8; 3:18; Rom. 12:2)
σοφίαν δὲ οὐ τοῦ αἰῶνος τούτου οὐδὲ τῶν ἀρχόντων τοῦ αἰῶνος τούτου τῶν καταργουμένων·

Rom. 8:38b
οὔτε ἄγγελοι οὔτε ἀρχαὶ οὔτε ἐνεστῶτα οὔτε μέλλοντα οὔτε δυνάμεις

I Cor. 15:27a
"πάντα" γὰρ "ὑπέταξεν ὑπὸ τοὺς πόδας αὐτοῦ."

Cf. I Cor. 15:27, 28; Phil. 2:10

Rom. 12:5a
οὕτως οἱ πολλοὶ ἓν σῶμά ἐσμεν ἐν Χριστῷ,

I Cor. 12:27a
ὑμεῖς δέ ἐστε σῶμα Χριστοῦ

Rom. 11:36a
ὅτι ἐξ αὐτοῦ καὶ δι' αὐτοῦ καὶ εἰς αὐτὸν τὰ πάντα·

I Cor. 15:28b
ἵνα ᾖ ὁ θεὸς πάντα ἐν πᾶσιν.

Cf. Rom. 6:11b
νεκροὺς μὲν τῇ ἁμαρτίᾳ

EPHESIANS 2	COLOSSIAN PARALLELS
κατὰ τὸν αἰῶνα τοῦ κόσμου τούτου,	
κατὰ τὸν ἄρχοντα τῆς ἐξουσίας τοῦ ἀέρος,	1:13a ὃς ἐρύσατο ἡμᾶς ἐκ τῆς ἐξουσίας τοῦ σκότους
τοῦ πνεύματος τοῦ νῦν ἐνεργοῦντος	
ἐν τοῖς υἱοῖς τῆς ἀπειθίας·	
3 ἐν οἷς καὶ ἡμεῖς πάντες	3:7 ἐν οἷς καὶ ὑμεῖς
ἀνεστράφημέν ποτε	περιεπατήσατέ ποτε ὅτε ἐζῆτε ἐν τούτοις·
ἐν ταῖς ἐπιθυμίαις τῆς σαρκὸς ἡμῶν,	
ποιοῦντες τὰ θελήματα τῆς σαρκὸς καὶ τῶν διανοιῶν,	1:21 καὶ ὑμᾶς ποτὲ ὄντας ἀπηλλοτριωμένους καὶ ἐχθροὺς τῇ διανοίᾳ ἐν τοῖς ἔργοις τοῖς πονηροῖς,—
καὶ ἤμεθα τέκνα φύσει ὀργῆς	Cf. 3:6 ἡ ὀργὴ τοῦ θεοῦ
ὡς καὶ οἱ λοιποί·—	

Other Pauline Parallels

Rom. 12:2a
καὶ μὴ συνσχηματίζεσθε τῷ αἰῶνι τούτῳ,

I Cor. 2:12b
οὐ τὸ πνεῦμα τοῦ κόσμου ἐλάβομεν

Cf. II Thess. 2:3b, 4a
ὁ ἄνθρωπος τῆς ἀνομίας,
ὁ υἱὸς τῆς ἀπωλείας, ὁ ἀντικείμενος

Cf. I Cor. 2:6, 8.

II Thess. 2:7a
τὸ γὰρ μυστήριον ἤδη ἐνεργεῖται τῆς ἀνομίας·

I Thess. 2:13b
ὃς καὶ ἐνεργεῖται

Rom. 15:31a; cf. 11:30
ἵνα ῥυσθῶ ἀπὸ τῶν ἀπειθούντων ἐν τῇ Ἰουδαίᾳ

ἐν ὑμῖν τοῖς πιστεύουσιν.

Rom. 3:23; cf. 3:9
πάντες γὰρ ἥμαρτον καὶ ὑστεροῦνται τῆς δόξης τοῦ θεοῦ,

II Cor. 1:12b
ἀνεστράφημεν ἐν τῷ κόσμῳ

Rom. 13:14b; cf. Gal. 5:16, 24
καὶ τῆς σαρκὸς πρόνοιαν μὴ ποιεῖσθε εἰς ἐπιθυμίας.

Rom. 1:24b
ἐν ταῖς ἐπιθυμίαις τῶν καρδιῶν αὐτῶν

Rom. 8:7; cf. Gal. 5:19
διότι τὸ φρόνημα τῆς σαρκὸς ἔχθρα εἰς θεόν,

I Thess. 5:9a
ὅτι οὐκ ἔθετο ἡμᾶς ὁ θεὸς εἰς ὀργὴν

Gal. 4:28b
ἐπαγγελίας τέκνα ἐσμέν·

Cf. Gal. 2:15a
Ἡμεῖς φύσει Ἰουδαῖοι

I Thess. 4:13b
καθὼς καὶ οἱ λοιποὶ

EPHESIANS 2	Colossian Parallels
4 ὁ δὲ θεὸς πλούσιος ὢν ἐν ἐλέει,	
διὰ τὴν πολλὴν ἀγάπην αὐτοῦ	
ἣν ἠγάπησεν ἡμᾶς,	2:13, cf. 12
5 καὶ ὄντας ἡμᾶς νεκροὺς τοῖς παραπτώμασιν	καὶ ὑμᾶς νεκροὺς ὄντας τοῖς παραπτώμασιν . . . .
συνεζωοποίησεν τῷ χριστῷ,—	συνεζωοποίησεν ὑμᾶς σὺν αὐτῷ·
χάριτί ἐστε σεσωσμένοι,—	
	2:12a
6 καὶ συνήγειρεν	ἐν ᾧ καὶ συνηγέρθητε
	3:1
	Εἰ οὖν συνηγέρθητε τῷ χριστῷ, τὰ ἄνω ζητεῖτε, οὗ ὁ χριστός ἐστιν
καὶ συνεκάθισεν ἐν τοῖς ἐπουρανίοις	"ἐν δεξιᾷ τοῦ θεοῦ" καθήμενος·
	3:3
	ἀπεθάνετε γάρ, καὶ ἡ ζωὴ ὑμῶν κέκρυπται σὺν τῷ χριστῷ ἐν τῷ θεῷ·
ἐν Χριστῷ Ἰησοῦ,	See 3:1 above
7 ἵνα ἐνδείξηται ἐν τοῖς αἰῶσιν τοῖς ἐπερχομένοις τὸ ὑπερβάλλον πλοῦτος τῆς χάριτος αὐτοῦ ἐν χρηστότητι ἐφ' ἡμᾶς ἐν Χριστῷ Ἰησοῦ.	Cf. 1:4 above

Other Pauline Parallels

Rom. 11:32b, 33a

ἵνα τοὺς πάντας ἐλεήσῃ. Ὦ βάθος πλούτου καὶ σοφίας καὶ γνώσεως θεοῦ·

Rom. 5:8; cf. 5:5; 8:39

συνίστησιν δὲ τὴν ἑαυτοῦ ἀγάπην εἰς ἡμᾶς ὁ θεὸς ὅτι ἔτι ἁμαρτωλῶν ὄντων ἡμῶν Χριστὸς ὑπὲρ ἡμῶν ἀπέθανεν.

II Thess. 2:16b

ὁ ἀγαπήσας ἡμᾶς

Cf. Rom. 8:10

Rom. 3:24a

δικαιούμενοι δωρεὰν τῇ αὐτοῦ χάριτι

Cf. Rom. 6:5, 8, 11

Cf. Phil. 3:20, 2:10   Cf. I Cor. 15:40

Rom. 9:23a

ἵνα γνωρίσῃ
                                      Rom. 2:4a

τὸν πλοῦτον τῆς δόξης αὐτοῦ   ἢ τοῦ πλούτου (Cf. II Cor. 9:14)
ἐπὶ σκεύη ἐλέους,
                                      τῆς χρηστότητος αὐτοῦ . . . .
                                      καταφρονεῖς,

EPHESIANS 2	Colossian Parallels
8 τῇ γὰρ χάριτί ἐστε σεσωσμένοι	
διὰ πίστεως·	
καὶ τοῦτο οὐκ ἐξ ὑμῶν,	
θεοῦ τὸ δῶρον·	
9 οὐκ ἐξ ἔργων,	
ἵνα μή τις καυχήσηται.	
10 αὐτοῦ γάρ ἐσμεν ποίημα,	
κτισθέντες ἐν Χριστῷ Ἰησοῦ	Cf. 3:9, 10
	1:10a
	περιπατῆσαι ἀξίως τοῦ κυρίου
	. . . .
ἐπὶ ἔργοις ἀγαθοῖς	ἐν παντὶ ἔργῳ ἀγαθῷ καρποφοροῦντες
	Cf. 1:21b
	ἐν τοῖς ἔργοις τοῖς πονηροῖς,
οἷς προητοίμασεν ὁ θεὸς	
ἵνα ἐν αὐτοῖς περιπατήσωμεν.	Cf. 1:10a above

Other Pauline Parallels

Rom. 3:24; cf. chaps. 3–5

δικαιούμενοι δωρεὰν τῇ αὐτοῦ χάριτι διὰ τῆς ἀπολυτρώσεως τῆς ἐν Χριστῷ Ἰησοῦ·

Rom. 3:28

λογιζόμεθα γὰρ δικαιοῦσθαι πίστει ἄνθρωπον χωρὶς ἔργων νόμου. Cf. Gal. 2:16

Rom. 5:15b; cf. 3:24 above

ἡ χάρις τοῦ θεοῦ καὶ ἡ δωρεὰ ἐν χάριτι τῇ τοῦ ἑνὸς ἀνθρώπου Ἰησοῦ Χριστοῦ

Rom. 4:2; cf. 3:27

εἰ γὰρ Ἀβραὰμ ἐξ ἔργων ἐδικαιώθη, ἔχει καύχημα·

I Cor. 1:29, 30a

ὅπως μὴ καυχήσηται πᾶσα σὰρξ ἐνώπιον τοῦ θεοῦ.

ἐξ αὐτοῦ δὲ ὑμεῖς ἐστε ἐν Χριστῷ Ἰησοῦ,

II Cor. 5:17a; cf. Gal. 6:15

ὥστε εἴ τις ἐν Χριστῷ, καινὴ κτίσις·

Rom. 13:3a

οἱ γὰρ ἄρχοντες οὐκ εἰσὶν φόβος τῷ ἀγαθῷ ἔργῳ

Cf. Rom. 8:29a

ὅτι οὓς προέγνω, καὶ προώρισεν συμμόρφους τῆς εἰκόνος τοῦ υἱοῦ αὐτοῦ,

Rom. 8:24a

τῇ γὰρ ἐλπίδι ἐσώθημεν·

Rom. 9:32b

ὅτι οὐκ ἐκ πίστεως ἀλλ' ὡς ἐξ ἔργων·

Rom. 3:27

Ποῦ οὖν ἡ καύχησις; ἐξεκλείσθη. διὰ ποίου νόμου; τῶν ἔργων; οὐχί, ἀλλὰ διὰ νόμου πίστεως.

II Cor. 9:8b

εἰς πᾶν ἔργον ἀγαθόν·

EPHESIANS 2	Colossian Parallels
	4:18b
11 Διὸ μνημονεύετε ὅτι ποτὲ ὑμεῖς τὰ ἔθνη ἐν σαρκί,	μνημονεύετέ μου τῶν δεσμῶν.
οἱ λεγόμενοι	
ἀκροβυστία	
	Cf. 2:11
ὑπὸ τῆς λεγομένης περιτομῆς[14]	ἐν ᾧ καὶ περιετμήθητε περιτομῇ ἀχειροποιήτῳ
See vs. 10 above ἐν σαρκὶ χειροποιήτου,—	ἐν τῇ ἀπεκδύσει τοῦ σώματος τῆς σαρκός, ἐν τῇ περιτομῇ τοῦ χριστοῦ,
	1:21a
12 ὅτι ἦτε τῷ καιρῷ ἐκείνῳ χωρὶς Χριστοῦ,	καὶ ὑμᾶς ποτὲ ὄντας
ἀπηλλοτριωμένοι τῆς πολιτείας τοῦ Ἰσραὴλ καὶ ξένοι τῶν διαθηκῶν τῆς ἐπαγγελίας,	ἀπηλλοτριωμένους
ἐλπίδα μὴ ἔχοντες	
καὶ ἄθεοι	
ἐν τῷ κόσμῳ.	

Other Pauline Parallels

I Cor. 12:2a
Οἴδατε ὅτι ὅτε ἔθνη ἦτε

Cf. I Cor. 8:5a
καὶ γὰρ εἴπερ εἰσὶν λεγόμενοι θεοὶ
See below

Gal. 6:15
οὔτε γὰρ περιτομή τι ἔστιν
οὔτε ἀκροβυστία,
ἀλλὰ καινὴ κτίσις.

Cf. Rom. 1:28-32

Rom. 9:4
οἵτινές εἰσιν Ἰσραηλεῖται,
ὧν . . . . αἱ διαθῆκαι . . . .
καὶ αἱ ἐπαγγελίαι,

I Thess. 4:13b
καθὼς καὶ οἱ λοιποὶ οἱ μὴ ἔχοντες ἐλπίδα.

I Thess. 4:5b
καθάπερ καὶ "τὰ ἔθνη τὰ μὴ εἰδότα τὸν θεόν,"

Cf. I Cor. 4:9b
ὅτι θέατρον ἐγενήθημεν τῷ κόσμῳ

Cf. Rom. 11:17

Rom. 2:28b; cf. vss. 26-29
οὐδὲ ἡ ἐν τῷ φανερῷ

ἐν σαρκὶ περιτομή·

Gal. 5:4a
κατηργήθητε ἀπὸ Χριστοῦ

Gal. 4:8, 9a
Ἀλλὰ τότε μὲν οὐκ εἰδότες θεὸν ἐδουλεύσατε τοῖς φύσει μὴ οὖσι θεοῖς·

[14] Phil. 3:3, ἡμεῖς γάρ ἐσμεν ἡ περιτομή, οἱ οὐκ ἐν σαρκὶ πεποιθότες.

EPHESIANS 2	Colossian Parallels
	1:22a; cf. 3:11
13 νυνὶ δὲ ἐν Χριστῷ Ἰησοῦ ὑμεῖς οἵ ποτε ὄντες "μακρὰν"[15] ἐγενήθητε "ἐγγὺς" ἐν τῷ αἵματι τοῦ χριστοῦ.	νυνὶ δὲ ἀποκατήλλαξεν ἐν τῷ σώματι τῆς σαρκὸς αὐτοῦ διὰ τοῦ θανάτου,—
	1:20b
14 Αὐτὸς γάρ ἐστιν ἡ "εἰρήνη" ἡμῶν,[16]	εἰρηνοποιήσας διὰ τοῦ αἵματος τοῦ σταυροῦ αὐτοῦ,
ὁ ποιήσας τὰ ἀμφότερα ἓν	
καὶ τὸ μεσότοιχον τοῦ φραγμοῦ λύσας, τὴν ἔχθραν	1:21b ἐχθροὺς τῇ διανοίᾳ
ἐν τῇ σαρκὶ αὐτοῦ,	
	2:14a
15 τὸν νόμον τῶν ἐντολῶν ἐν δόγμασιν καταργήσας,	ἐξαλείψας τὸ καθ' ἡμῶν χειρόγραφον τοῖς δόγμασιν ὃ ἦν ὑπεναντίον ἡμῖν, See above
ἵνα τοὺς δύο κτίσῃ ἐν αὐτῷ	

[15] Cf. Isa. 57:19, εἰρήνην ἐπ' εἰρήνην τοῖς μακρὰν καὶ τοῖς ἐγγὺς οὖσιν.

[16] Cf. Mic. 5:5 (4), καὶ ἔσται αὕτη εἰρήνη. See Isa. 57:19 above.

Other Pauline Parallels

Gal. 3:28b; cf. 28a
πάντες γὰρ ὑμεῖς εἷς ἐστὲ
ἐν Χριστῷ Ἰησοῦ.

νῦν δὲ γνόντες θεόν, ...

Rom. 5:1b, 2a
εἰρήνην ἔχωμεν πρὸς τὸν θεὸν
διὰ τοῦ κυρίου ἡμῶν Ἰησοῦ Χριστοῦ, δι' οὗ καὶ τὴν προσαγωγὴν
ἐσχήκαμεν

Gal. 3:28c
πάντες γὰρ ὑμεῖς εἷς ἐστὲ ἐν
Χριστῷ Ἰησοῦ.

Gal. 3:28a
οὐκ ἔνι Ἰουδαῖος οὐδὲ Ἕλλην,

See Gal. 3:28 above

EPHESIANS 2	Colossian Parallels
	3:10a
εἰς ἕνα καινὸν ἄνθρωπον	καὶ ἐνδυσάμενοι τὸν νέον τὸν ἀνακαινούμενον
	1:20b
ποιῶν εἰρήνην,	εἰρηνοποιήσας
	1:22a
16 καὶ ἀποκαταλλάξῃ τοὺς ἀμφοτέρους[17]	νυνὶ δὲ ἀποκατήλλαξεν
ἐν ἑνὶ σώματι	ἐν τῷ σώματι τῆς σαρκὸς αὐτοῦ διὰ τοῦ θανάτου
τῷ θεῷ	See note 17
	1:20c
διὰ τοῦ σταυροῦ ἀποκτείνας τὴν ἔχθραν ἐν αὐτῷ·	διὰ τοῦ αἵματος τοῦ σταυροῦ αὐτοῦ
17 καὶ ἐλθὼν "εὐηγγελίσατο"[18] "εἰρήνην" ὑμῖν "τοῖς μακρὰν" "καὶ εἰρήνην τοῖς ἐγγύς·"[19]	
18 ὅτι δι' αὐτοῦ ἔχομεν τὴν προσαγωγὴν οἱ ἀμφότεροι	
ἐν ἑνὶ πνεύματι πρὸς τὸν πατέρα.	3:11a
19 "Ἄρα οὖν οὐκέτι ἐστὲ ξένοι καὶ πάροικοι,	ὅπου οὐκ ἔνι Ἕλλην καὶ Ἰουδαῖος, ... βάρβαρος, Σκύθης,
ἀλλὰ ἐστὲ συνπολῖται τῶν ἁγίων	
καὶ οἰκεῖοι τοῦ θεοῦ,	

[18] Isa. 52:7b, ὡς πόδες εὐαγγελιζομένου ἀκοὴν εἰρήνης.

[19] Isa. 57:19, εἰρήνην ἐπ' εἰρήνην τοῖς μακρὰν καὶ τοῖς ἐγγὺς οὖσιν.

[17] 1:20a, καὶ δι' αὐτοῦ ἀποκαταλλάξαι τὰ πάντα εἰς αὐτόν.

Other Pauline Parallels

II Cor. 5:17a ὥστε εἴ τις ἐν Χριστῷ, καινὴ κτίσις·	
	I Cor. 12:13b ἡμεῖς πάντες εἰς ἓν σῶμα ἐβαπτίσθημεν
Rom. 5:2a δι' οὗ καὶ τὴν προσαγωγὴν ἐσχήκαμεν	
Phil. 1:27b ἐν ἑνὶ πνεύματι,	I Cor. 12:13a καὶ γὰρ ἐν ἑνὶ πνεύματι
Phil. 3:20a ἡμῶν γὰρ τὸ πολίτευμα ἐν οὐρανοῖς ὑπάρχει,	
Gal. 6:10b μάλιστα δὲ πρὸς τοὺς οἰκείους τῆς πίστεως.	

EPHESIANS 2	COLOSSIAN PARALLELS
	2:7b
20 ἐποικοδομηθέντες ἐπὶ τῷ θεμελίῳ	καὶ ἐποικοδομούμενοι ἐν αὐτῷ
τῶν ἀποστόλων καὶ προφητῶν,[20]	
ὄντος "ἀκρογωνιαίου" αὐτοῦ Χριστοῦ Ἰησοῦ,	
21 ἐν ᾧ πᾶσα οἰκοδομὴ	
	2:19b
συναρμολογουμένη αὔξει	καὶ συνβιβαζόμενον αὔξει τὴν αὔξησιν τοῦ θεοῦ.
εἰς ναὸν ἅγιον	
	2:7b
ἐν κυρίῳ,	καὶ ἐποικοδομούμενοι ἐν αὐτῷ
22 ἐν ᾧ καὶ ὑμεῖς συνοικοδομεῖσθε	See above
εἰς κατοικητήριον τοῦ θεοῦ	
ἐν πνεύματι.	
3	
1 Τούτου χάριν ἐγὼ Παῦλος[21]	
ὁ δέσμιος τοῦ χριστοῦ Ἰησοῦ	
	1:24a
ὑπὲρ ὑμῶν τῶν ἐθνῶν,—	Νῦν χαίρω ἐν τοῖς παθήμασιν ὑπὲρ ὑμῶν,

[20] Acts 13:1b, προφῆται καὶ διδάσκαλοι. Acts 15:6b, οἱ ἀπόστολοι καὶ οἱ πρεσβύτεροι. Cf. Rev. 18:20, καὶ οἱ ἅγιοι καὶ οἱ ἀπόστολοι καὶ οἱ προφῆται.

Other Pauline Parallels

I Cor. 3:11b
θεμέλιον γὰρ ἄλλον οὐδεὶς δύναται θεῖναι

παρὰ τὸν κείμενον, ὅς ἐστιν Ἰησοῦς Χριστός·

I Cor. 3:9b
θεοῦ οἰκοδομή ἐστε.

I Cor. 3:6b, 7b
ἀλλὰ ὁ θεὸς ηὔξανεν· . . . . ἀλλ' ὁ αὐξάνων θεός.

I Cor. 3:16a, 17b
Οὐκ οἴδατε ὅτι ναὸς θεοῦ ἐστε . . . . ὁ γὰρ ναὸς τοῦ θεοῦ ἅγιός ἐστιν, οἵτινές ἐστε ὑμεῖς.

I Cor. 3:10b,12a, 16b
ἄλλος δὲ ἐποικοδομεῖ. ἕκαστος δὲ βλεπέτω πῶς ἐποικοδομεῖ· . . . . εἰ δέ τις ἐποικοδομεῖ . . . . καὶ τὸ πνεῦμα τοῦ θεοῦ ἐν ὑμῖν οἰκεῖ;

Rom. 8:9
Ὑμεῖς δὲ οὐκ ἐστὲ ἐν σαρκὶ ἀλλὰ ἐν πνεύματι, εἴπερ πνεῦμα θεοῦ οἰκεῖ ἐν ὑμῖν.

II Cor. 10:1
Αὐτὸς δὲ ἐγὼ Παῦλος

Philem. 1
ΠΑΥΛΟΣ δέσμιος Χριστοῦ Ἰησοῦ

Rom. 11:13a
Ὑμῖν δὲ λέγω τοῖς ἔθνεσιν.

I Cor. 12:28a
Καὶ οὓς μὲν ἔθετο ὁ θεὸς ἐν τῇ ἐκκλησίᾳ
πρῶτον ἀποστόλους, δεύτερον προφήτας,

II Cor. 6:16b
ἡμεῖς γὰρ ναὸς

θεοῦ ἐσμεν ζῶντος·

---

[21] Gal. 5:2a, Ἴδε ἐγὼ Παῦλος λέγω ὑμῖν.

EPHESIANS 3	Colossian Parallels
2 εἴ γε ἠκούσατε	
	1:25b
τὴν οἰκονομίαν τῆς χάριτος τοῦ θεοῦ	κατὰ τὴν οἰκονομίαν τοῦ θεοῦ
τῆς δοθείσης μοι εἰς ὑμᾶς,	τὴν δοθεῖσάν μοι εἰς ὑμᾶς
3 [ὅτι] κατὰ ἀποκάλυψιν	
ἐγνωρίσθη μοι	
τὸ μυστήριον,	Cf. 1:26
καθὼς προέγραψα ἐν ὀλίγῳ,	
4 πρὸς ὃ δύνασθε ἀναγινώσκοντες	4:16a καὶ ὅταν ἀναγνωσθῇ παρ' ὑμῖν ἡ ἐπιστολή,
	1:9b
νοῆσαι τὴν σύνεσίν μου	ἵνα πληρωθῆτε τὴν ἐπίγνωσιν τοῦ θελήματος αὐτοῦ ἐν πάσῃ σοφίᾳ καὶ συνέσει πνευματικῇ,
	4:3b
ἐν τῷ μυστηρίῳ τοῦ χριστοῦ,[22]	τὸ μυστήριον τοῦ χριστοῦ
	1:26b
5 ὃ ἑτέραις γενεαῖς οὐκ ἐγνωρίσθη	τὸ ἀποκεκρυμμένον ἀπὸ τῶν αἰώνων καὶ ἀπὸ τῶν γενεῶν,—
τοῖς υἱοῖς τῶν ἀνθρώπων[23] ὡς νῦν ἀπεκαλύφθη	νῦν δὲ ἐφανερώθη

[23] Cf. Mark 3:28, τοῖς υἱοῖς τῶν ἀνθρώπων.

[22] 1:25 b, πληρῶσαι τὸν λόγον τοῦ θεοῦ.

Other Pauline Parallels

Gal. 1:13
Ἠκούσατε γὰρ τὴν ἐμὴν ἀναστροφήν ποτε

I Cor. 9:17b; cf. 4:1
εἰ δὲ ἄκων, οἰκονομίαν πεπίστευμαι.

Gal. 2:9
τὴν χάριν τὴν δοθεῖσάν μοι

I Cor. 2:10
ἡμῖν γὰρ ἀπεκάλυψεν ὁ θεὸς διὰ τοῦ πνεύματος,

Gal. 1:12
οὐδὲ γὰρ ἐγὼ παρὰ ἀνθρώπου παρέλαβον αὐτό, οὔτε ἐδιδάχθην, ἀλλὰ δι' ἀποκαλύψεως Ἰησοῦ Χριστοῦ.
Cf. Gal. 1:16
Cf. Rom. 11:25; I Cor. 2:7; 4:1

I Cor. 5:9a
Ἔγραψα ὑμῖν ἐν τῇ ἐπιστολῇ
Cf. Gal. 1:12, 16; 2:2, 7, 8

II Cor. 11:6b
ἀλλ' οὐ τῇ γνώσει, ἀλλ' ἐν παντὶ φανερώσαντες ἐν πᾶσιν εἰς ὑμᾶς.

I Cor. 2:7, 8a
ἀλλὰ λαλοῦμεν θεοῦ σοφίαν ἐν μυστηρίῳ,
τὴν ἀποκεκρυμμένην, ...
ἣν οὐδεὶς τῶν ἀρχόντων τοῦ αἰῶνος τούτου ἔγνωκεν,

I Cor. 2:10 above

I Cor. 1:4b; cf. Rom. 12:6; 15:15
ἐπὶ τῇ χάριτι τοῦ θεοῦ

τῇ δοθείσῃ ὑμῖν

Rom. 16:25b; cf. Gal. 2:2b
κατὰ ἀποκάλυψιν

μυστηρίου

Rom. 16:25b, 26a
κατὰ ἀποκάλυψιν μυστηρίου

χρόνοις αἰωνίοις
σεσιγημένου

φανερωθέντος δὲ νῦν

EPHESIANS 3	COLOSSIAN PARALLELS
τοῖς ἁγίοις ἀποστόλοις αὐτοῦ	τοῖς ἁγίοις αὐτοῦ,
καὶ προφήταις	
	1:8
	ὁ καὶ δηλώσας ἡμῖν τὴν ὑμῶν ἀγάπην
ἐν πνεύματι,	ἐν πνεύματι.
6 εἶναι τὰ ἔθνη συνκληρονόμα	
καὶ σύνσωμα	
καὶ συνμέτοχα τῆς ἐπαγγελίας	
ἐν Χριστῷ Ἰησοῦ	
διὰ τοῦ εὐαγγελίου,	

Other Pauline Parallels

I Cor. 12:28b
πρῶτον ἀποστόλους,

δεύτερον προφήτας,

I Cor. 14:16a
ἐπεὶ ἐὰν εὐλογῇς [ἐν] πνεύματι,
Cf. I Cor. 2:10 above

Rom. 8:17b
κληρονόμοι μὲν θεοῦ, συνκληρονόμοι δὲ Χριστοῦ,

Rom. 12:5
οὕτως οἱ πολλοὶ ἓν σῶμά ἐσμεν ἐν Χριστῷ,

Rom. 4:13, 14, 16, 17
Οὐ γὰρ διὰ νόμου ἡ ἐπαγγελία τῷ Ἀβραὰμ ἢ τῷ cπέρματι αὐτοῦ, τὸ κληρονόμον αὐτὸν εἶναι κόσμου, ἀλλὰ διὰ δικαιοσύνης πίστεως· εἰ γὰρ οἱ ἐκ νόμου κληρονόμοι, κεκένωται ἡ πίστις καὶ κατήργηται ἡ ἐπαγγελία·
.... Διὰ τοῦτο ἐκ πίστεως, ἵνα κατὰ χάριν, εἰς τὸ εἶναι βεβαίαν τὴν ἐπαγγελίαν παντὶ τῷ σπέρματι, οὐ τῷ ἐκ τοῦ νόμου μόνον ἀλλὰ καὶ τῷ ἐκ πίστεως Ἀβραάμ, (ὅς ἐστιν πατὴρ πάντων ἡμῶν, καθὼς γέγραπται ὅτι "Πατέρα πολλῶν ἐθνῶν τέθεικά σε,)

II Thess. 2:14b
διὰ τοῦ εὐαγγελίου ἡμῶν,

Rom. 16:26b
διά τε γραφῶν προφητικῶν ....
εἰς πάντα τὰ ἔθνη γνωρισθέντος,

Gal. 3:26–29
Πάντες γὰρ υἱοὶ θεοῦ ἐστὲ διὰ τῆς πίστεως ἐν Χριστῷ Ἰησοῦ. ὅσοι γὰρ εἰς Χριστὸν ἐβαπτίσθητε, Χριστὸν ἐνεδύσασθε· οὐκ ἔνι Ἰουδαῖος οὐδὲ Ἕλλην, οὐκ ἔνι δοῦλος οὐδὲ ἐλεύθερος, οὐκ ἔνι ἄρσεν καὶ θῆλυ· πάντες γὰρ ὑμεῖς εἷς ἐστὲ ἐν Χριστῷ Ἰησοῦ. εἰ δὲ ὑμεῖς Χριστοῦ, ἄρα τοῦ Ἀβραὰμ σπέρμα ἐστέ, κατ' ἐπαγγελίαν κληρονόμοι.

EPHESIANS 3	Colossian Parallels
7 οὗ ἐγενήθην διάκονος	1:23b οὗ ἐγενόμην ἐγὼ Παῦλος διάκονος. 1:25 ἧς ἐγενόμην ἐγὼ διάκονος
κατὰ τὴν δωρεὰν τῆς χάριτος τοῦ θεοῦ τῆς δοθείσης μοι	κατὰ τὴν οἰκονομίαν τοῦ θεοῦ τὴν δοθεῖσάν μοι 1:29b
κατὰ τὴν ἐνέργειαν τῆς δυνάμεως αὐτοῦ—	κατὰ τὴν ἐνέργειαν αὐτοῦ τὴν ἐνεργουμένην ἐν ἐμοὶ ἐν δυνάμει.
8 ἐμοὶ τῷ ἐλαχιστοτέρῳ πάντων ἁγίων	
ἐδόθη ἡ χάρις αὕτη—	
τοῖς ἔθνεσιν εὐαγγελίσασθαι	1:27 οἷς ἠθέλησεν ὁ θεὸς γνωρίσαι
τὸ ἀνεξιχνίαστον πλοῦτος τοῦ χριστοῦ,	τί τὸ πλοῦτος τῆς δόξης τοῦ μυστηρίου τούτου ἐν τοῖς ἔθνεσιν, ὅ ἐστιν Χριστὸς ἐν ὑμῖν, ἡ ἐλπὶς τῆς δόξης·
9 καὶ φωτίσαι τίς ἡ οἰκονομία	1:25b, 26 κατὰ τὴν οἰκονομίαν τοῦ θεοῦ . . . . πληρῶσαι τὸν λόγον τοῦ θεοῦ,
τοῦ μυστηρίου τοῦ ἀποκεκρυμμένου ἀπὸ τῶν αἰώνων	τὸ μυστήριον τὸ ἀποκεκρυμμένον ἀπὸ τῶν αἰώνων καὶ ἀπὸ τῶν γενεῶν,—

EPHESIANS AND THE PAULINE LETTERS

Other Pauline Parallels

Rom. 5:15b
ἡ χάρις τοῦ θεοῦ καὶ ἡ δωρεὰ ἐν χάριτι τῇ τοῦ ἑνὸς ἀνθρώπου Ἰησοῦ Χριστοῦ

εἰς τοὺς πολλοὺς ἐπερίσσευσεν.

I Cor. 15:9
Ἐγὼ γάρ εἰμι ὁ ἐλάχιστος τῶν ἀποστόλων, ὃς οὐκ εἰμὶ ἱκανὸς καλεῖσθαι ἀπόστολος,

Gal. 1:15b
καὶ "καλέσας" διὰ τῆς χάριτος αὐτοῦ
See Rom. 5:15b and 12:3 above

Gal. 1:16b
ἵνα εὐαγγελίζωμαι αὐτὸν ἐν τοῖς ἔθνεσιν,

Rom. 11:33
Ὦ βάθος πλούτου καὶ σοφίας καὶ γνώσεως θεοῦ· ὡς ἀνεξεραύνητα τὰ κρίματα αὐτοῦ
καὶ ἀνεξιχνίαστοι αἱ ὁδοὶ αὐτοῦ.

I Cor. 2:7
ἀλλὰ λαλοῦμεν θεοῦ σοφίαν

ἐν μυστηρίῳ, τὴν ἀποκεκρυμμένην,
ἣν προώρισεν ὁ θεὸς πρὸ τῶν αἰώνων εἰς δόξαν ἡμῶν·

Rom. 12:3, cf. 6
Λέγω γὰρ διὰ τῆς χάριτος τῆς δοθείσης μοι

Gal. 2:7b
ὅτι πεπίστευμαι

τὸ εὐαγγέλιον τῆς ἀκροβυστίας

Rom. 16:25b, 26
κατὰ ἀποκάλυψιν μυστηρίου

χρόνοις αἰωνίοις σεσιγημένου
φανερωθέντος δὲ νῦν
διά τε γραφῶν προφητικῶν

EPHESIANS 3	Colossian Parallels
ἐν τῷ θεῷ τῷ τὰ πάντα κτίσαντι,	3:3b καὶ ἡ ζωὴ ὑμῶν κέκρυπται σὺν τῷ χριστῷ ἐν τῷ θεῷ· 1:16b ἐν αὐτῷ ἐκτίσθη τὰ πάντα
10 ἵνα γνωρισθῇ νῦν	Cf. 1:27 above
	1:16c
ταῖς ἀρχαῖς καὶ ταῖς ἐξουσίαις	εἴτε ἀρχαὶ εἴτε ἐξουσίαι
	1:16b
ἐν τοῖς ἐπουρανίοις διὰ τῆς ἐκκλησίας	τὰ πάντα ἐν τοῖς οὐρανοῖς
ἡ πολυποίκιλος σοφία τοῦ θεοῦ,	
11 κατὰ πρόθεσιν τῶν αἰώνων	
ἣν ἐποίησεν ἐν τῷ χριστῷ Ἰησοῦ τῷ κυρίῳ ἡμῶν, 12 ἐν ᾧ ἔχομεν τὴν παρρησίαν	
καὶ προσαγωγὴν ἐν πεποιθήσει διὰ τῆς πίστεως αὐτοῦ.	
13 Διὸ αἰτοῦμαι μὴ ἐνκακεῖν ἐν ταῖς θλίψεσίν μου ὑπὲρ ὑμῶν,	1:24a Νῦν χαίρω ἐν τοῖς παθήμασιν ὑπὲρ ὑμῶν, 2:1 Θέλω γὰρ ὑμᾶς εἰδέναι ἡλίκον ἀγῶνα ἔχω ὑπὲρ ὑμῶν καὶ τῶν ἐν Λαοδικίᾳ καὶ ὅσοι οὐχ ἑόρακαν τὸ πρόσωπόν μου ἐν σαρκί,
ἥτις ἐστὶν δόξα ὑμῶν. 14 Τούτου χάριν κάμπτω τὰ γόνατά μου πρὸς τὸν πατέρα,	

Other Pauline Parallels

Rom. 11:36a
ὅτι ἐξ αὐτοῦ καὶ δι' αὐτοῦ καὶ εἰς αὐτὸν τὰ πάντα·

κατ' ἐπιταγὴν τοῦ αἰωνίου θεοῦ εἰς ὑπακοὴν πίστεως

εἰς πάντα τὰ ἔθνη γνωρισθέντος,

Cf. Rom. 8:38

II Cor. 8:18b
διὰ πασῶν τῶν ἐκκλησιῶν,—
See Rom. 11:33 above

I Cor. 2:7
ἀλλὰ λαλοῦμεν θεοῦ σοφίαν ἐν μυστηρίῳ, τὴν ἀποκεκρυμμένην,

Rom. 8:28b
τοῖς κατὰ πρόθεσιν κλητοῖς οὖσιν.

Rom. 5:1b, 2
διὰ τοῦ κυρίου ἡμῶν Ἰησοῦ Χριστοῦ,
δι' οὗ (cf. Phil. 1:20)

ἣν προώρισεν ὁ θεὸς πρὸ τῶν αἰώνων εἰς δόξαν ἡμῶν·

II Cor. 3:12
Ἔχοντες οὖν τοιαύτην ἐλπίδα πολλῇ παρρησίᾳ χρώμεθα,

II Cor. 3:4
Πεποίθησιν δὲ τοιαύτην ἔχομεν διὰ τοῦ χριστοῦ πρὸς τὸν θεόν.

καὶ τὴν προσαγωγὴν ἐσχήκαμεν

[τῇ πίστει] εἰς τὴν χάριν ταύτην ἐν ᾗ ἐστήκαμεν,

II Cor. 4:1, 16
οὐκ ἐγκακοῦμεν, ... Διὸ οὐκ ἐγκακοῦμεν,

I Thess. 2:20a
ὑμεῖς γάρ ἐστε ἡ δόξα ἡμῶν

Rom. 14:11 = Isa. 45:23
"ὅτι ἐμοὶ κάμψει πᾶν γόνυ".
cf. Phil. 2:10

EPHESIANS 3	Colossian Parallels
15 ἐξ οὗ πᾶσα πατριὰ[24] ἐν οὐρανοῖς καὶ ἐπὶ γῆς ὀνομάζεται, 16 ἵνα δῷ ὑμῖν κατὰ τὸ πλοῦτος τῆς δόξης αὐτοῦ[25] δυνάμει κραταιωθῆναι διὰ τοῦ πνεύματος αὐτοῦ εἰς τὸν ἔσω ἄνθρωπον, 17 κατοικῆσαι τὸν χριστὸν διὰ τῆς πίστεως ἐν ταῖς καρδίαις ὑμῶν ἐν ἀγάπῃ· ἐρριζωμένοι καὶ τεθεμελιωμένοι,	1:16b ἐν τοῖς οὐρανοῖς καὶ ἐπὶ τῆς γῆς, 1:27b γνωρίσαι τί τὸ πλοῦτος τῆς δόξης τοῦ μυστηρίου τούτου 1:19; cf. 2:9 κατοικῆσαι 2:7a ἐρριζωμένοι καὶ ἐποικοδομούμενοι ἐν αὐτῷ 1:23a εἴ γε ἐπιμένετε τῇ πίστει τεθεμελιωμένοι

[24] Acts 3:25 (=Gen. 12:3), "πᾶσαι αἱ πατριαὶ τῆς γῆς." Cf. Ps. 95 (96):7, αἱ πατριαὶ τῶν ἐθνῶν.

[25] 1:11a, ἐν πάσῃ δυνάμει δυναμούμενοι κατὰ τὸ κράτος τῆς δόξης αὐτοῦ.

Other Pauline Parallels

I Cor. 8:5b
εἴτε ἐν οὐρανῷ εἴτε ἐπὶ γῆς,

Rom. 15:20b
οὐχ ὅπου ὠνομάσθη Χριστός,

Rom. 9:23a
ἵνα γνωρίσῃ τὸν πλοῦτον τῆς δόξης αὐτοῦ

I Cor. 16:13b
ἀνδρίζεσθε, κραταιοῦσθε.

Rom. 15:13b, 19b
ἐν δυνάμει πνεύματος ἁγίου.

Rom. 7:22
κατὰ τὸν ἔσω ἄνθρωπον,

II Cor. 4:16
ἀλλ' εἰ καὶ ὁ ἔξω ἡμῶν ἄνθρωπος διαφθείρεται, ἀλλ' ὁ ἔσω ἡμῶν ἀνακαινοῦται ἡμέρᾳ καὶ ἡμέρᾳ.

Rom. 8:9b
εἴπερ πνεῦμα θεοῦ οἰκεῖ ἐν ὑμῖν.

I Cor. 3:16b
καὶ τὸ πνεῦμα τοῦ θεοῦ ἐν ὑμῖν οἰκεῖ;

II Cor. 1:22b; cf. 13:5
καὶ δοὺς τὸν ἀρραβῶνα τοῦ πνεύματος
ἐν ταῖς καρδίαις ἡμῶν.

II Cor. 13:5b
ὅτι Ἰησοῦς Χριστὸς

ἐν ὑμῖν

EPHESIANS 3	Colossian Parallels
	2:2b, 3; cf. 1:26
18 ἵνα ἐξισχύσητε καταλαβέσθαι	καὶ εἰς πᾶν πλοῦτος τῆς πληροφορίας τῆς συνέσεως,
σὺν πᾶσιν τοῖς ἁγίοις	
τί τὸ πλάτος καὶ μῆκος	εἰς ἐπίγνωσιν τοῦ μυστηρίου τοῦ θεοῦ, Χριστοῦ,
καὶ ὕψος καὶ βάθος,	
19 γνῶναί τε τὴν ὑπερβάλλουσαν τῆς γνώσεως	ἐν ᾧ εἰσὶν πάντες "οἱ θησαυροὶ τῆς σοφίας" καὶ γνώσεως "ἀπόκρυφοι."
ἀγάπην τοῦ χριστοῦ,	
	1:9b
ἵνα πληρωθῆτε	ἵνα πληρωθῆτε
	2:9
εἰς πᾶν τὸ πλήρωμα τοῦ θεοῦ.	ὅτι ἐν αὐτῷ κατοικεῖ πᾶν τὸ πλήρωμα τῆς θεότητος σωματικῶς, καὶ ἐστὲ ἐν αὐτῷ πεπληρωμένοι,
20 Τῷ δὲ δυναμένῳ ὑπὲρ πάντα ποιῆσαι	
ὑπερεκπερισσοῦ	
ὧν αἰτούμεθα ἢ νοοῦμεν	1:29b
κατὰ τὴν δύναμιν	κατὰ τὴν ἐνέργειαν αὐτοῦ
τὴν ἐνεργουμένην ἐν ἡμῖν,	τὴν ἐνεργουμένην ἐν ἐμοὶ ἐν δυνάμει.

Other Pauline Parallels

I Cor. 9:24b
οὕτως τρέχετε ἵνα καταλάβητε.

II Cor. 1:1b
σὺν τοῖς ἁγίοις πᾶσιν τοῖς οὖσιν ἐν ὅλῃ τῇ Ἀχαΐᾳ·

Rom. 3:38b
οὔτε δυνάμεις οὔτε ὕψωμα οὔτε βάθος

II Cor. 9:14
διὰ τὴν ὑπερβάλλουσαν χάριν τοῦ θεοῦ

I Cor. 8:2
ἡ γνῶσις φυσιοῖ, ἡ δὲ ἀγάπη οἰκοδομεῖ.

I Cor. 13:2, 8
κἂν ἔχω προφητείαν καὶ εἰδῶ τὰ μυστήρια πάντα καὶ πᾶσαν τὴν γνῶσιν, κἂν ἔχω πᾶσαν τὴν πίστιν ὥστε ὄρη μεθιστάνειν, ἀγάπην δὲ μὴ ἔχω οὐθέν εἰμι. . . . . Ἡ ἀγάπη οὐδέτοτε πίπτει. . . . . εἴτε γνῶσις, καταργηθήσεται.

Rom. 8:35a
τίς ἡμᾶς χωρίσει

ἀπὸ τῆς ἀγάπης τοῦ χριστοῦ;

Rom. 16:25a
Τῷ δὲ δυναμένῳ ὑμᾶς στηρίξαι

I Thess. 3:10b
ὑπερεκπερισσοῦ δεόμενοι

Gal. 3:5b; cf. Phil. 3:21
καὶ ἐνεργῶν δυνάμεις ἐν ὑμῖν

EPHESIANS 3	Colossian Parallels
21 αὐτῷ ἡ δόξα	
ἐν τῇ ἐκκλησίᾳ	
καὶ ἐν Χριστῷ Ἰησοῦ	1:26b
εἰς πάσας τὰς γενεὰς	ἀπὸ τῶν αἰώνων
τοῦ αἰῶνος τῶν αἰώνων· ἀμήν.	καὶ ἀπὸ τῶν γενεῶν,
4	
1 Παρακαλῶ οὖν ὑμᾶς ἐγὼ	
ὁ δέσμιος ἐν κυρίῳ	
	1:10a
περιπατῆσαι ἀξίως	περιπατῆσαι ἀξίως τοῦ κυρίου
τῆς κλήσεως ἧς ἐκλήθητε,[26]	
	3:12, 13a
2 μετὰ πάσης ταπεινοφροσύνης	Ἐνδύσασθε οὖν .... ταπεινοφροσύνην,
καὶ πραΰτητος,	πραΰτητα,
μετὰ μακροθυμίας,	μακροθυμίαν,
ἀνεχόμενοι ἀλλήλων	ἀνεχόμενοι ἀλλήλων
	3:14, 15
ἐν ἀγάπῃ,	ἐπὶ πᾶσι δὲ τούτοις τὴν ἀγάπην,
3 σπουδάζοντες τηρεῖν	
τὴν ἑνότητα τοῦ πνεύματος	
ἐν τῷ συνδέσμῳ	ὅ ἐστιν σύνδεσμος τῆς τελειότητος.
τῆς εἰρήνης·	καὶ ἡ εἰρήνη τοῦ χριστοῦ

Other Pauline Parallels

Rom. 11:36b   Rom. 16:27b
αὐτῷ ἡ δόξα   [ᾧ] ἡ δόξα

I Cor. 6:4b
ἐν τῇ ἐκκλησίᾳ

Rom. 3:24b
ἐν Χριστῷ Ἰησοῦ

Rom. 11:36c   Rom. 16:27c
εἰς τοὺς αἰῶνας·   εἰς τοὺς αἰῶνας·
ἀμήν.   ἀμήν.

Rom. 12:1a
Παρακαλῶ οὖν ὑμᾶς,

Philem. 1, 9
δέσμιος Χριστοῦ Ἰησοῦ

I Thess. 2:12b
εἰς τὸ περιπατεῖν ὑμᾶς ἀξίως
τοῦ θεοῦ τοῦ καλοῦντος ὑμᾶς

Phil. 2:3b
ἀλλὰ τῇ ταπεινοφροσύνῃ

ἀλλήλους ἡγούμενοι ὑπερέχοντας
ἑαυτῶν,

Phil. 2:2b
ἵνα τὸ αὐτὸ φρονῆτε,
τὴν αὐτὴν ἀγάπην ἔχοντες,

σύνψυχοι, τὸ ἓν φρονοῦντες,

Gal. 1:5a
ᾧ ἡ δόξα

I Cor. 7:17b
ἐν ταῖς ἐκκλησίαις πάσαις

Gal. 1:5b
εἰς
τοὺς αἰῶνας τῶν αἰώνων· ἀμήν.

II Cor. 10:1a
Αὐτὸς δὲ ἐγὼ Παῦλος
παρακαλῶ ὑμᾶς

Phil. 1:13b
τοὺς δεσμούς μου .... ἐν Χριστῷ

II Thess. 1:11b
ἵνα ὑμᾶς ἀξιώσῃ
τῆς κλήσεως ὁ θεὸς ἡμῶν

I Thess. 4:9b
εἰς τὸ ἀγαπᾶν ἀλλήλους·

---

[26] I Cor. 7:20, ἕκαστος ἐν τῇ κλήσει ᾗ ἐκλήθη ἐν ταύτῃ μενέτω.

EPHESIANS 4	Colossian Parallels
4 ἓν σῶμα	βραβευέτω ἐν ταῖς καρδίαις ὑμῶν, εἰς ἣν καὶ ἐκλήθητε ἐν [ἑνὶ] σώματι·
καὶ ἓν πνεῦμα	
καθὼς [καὶ] ἐκλήθητε ἐν μιᾷ ἐλπίδι τῆς κλήσεως ὑμῶν·	
See below	
5 εἷς κύριος, μία πίστις, ἓν βάπτισμα·	
6 εἷς θεὸς καὶ πατὴρ πάντων, ὁ ἐπὶ πάντων καὶ διὰ πάντων καὶ ἐν πᾶσιν.	
7 Ἑνὶ δὲ ἑκάστῳ ἡμῶν ἐδόθη [ἡ] χάρις κατὰ τὸ μέτρον τῆς δωρεᾶς τοῦ χριστοῦ.	
8 διὸ λέγει "'Ἀναβὰς εἰς ὕψος ᾐχμαλώτευσεν αἰχμαλωσίαν, [καὶ] ἔδωκεν δόματα τοῖς ἀνθρώποις."[27]	Cf. 2:15

[27] Ps. 67 (68):19, ἀναβὰς εἰς ὕψος ᾐχμαλώτευσας αἰχμαλωσίαν, ἔλαβες δόματα ἐν ἀνθρώπῳ.

Other Pauline Parallels

I Cor. 10:17*b*
ἓν σῶμα οἱ πολλοί ἐσμεν,

I Cor. 12:13
καὶ γὰρ ἐν ἑνὶ πνεύματι ἡμεῖς πάντες
εἰς ἓν σῶμα ἐβαπτίσθημεν, ...
καὶ πάντες ἓν πνεῦμα ἐποτίσθημεν.

I Cor. 7:20
ἕκαστος ἐν τῇ κλήσει ᾗ ἐκλήθη
ἐν ταύτῃ μενέτω.

I Cor. 8:6*a*
[ἀλλ'] ἡμῖν εἷς θεὸς ὁ πατήρ,
ἐξ οὗ τὰ πάντα καὶ ἡμεῖς εἰς αὐτόν,
καὶ εἷς κύριος Ἰησοῦς Χριστός,
See I Cor. 12:13 above, cf. 1:13

Rom. 3:30*b*
εἴπερ εἷς ὁ θεός,

Rom. 11:36*a*
ὅτι ἐξ αὐτοῦ καὶ δι' αὐτοῦ
καὶ εἰς αὐτὸν τὰ πάντα·

Rom. 12:6*a*
Ἔχοντες δὲ χαρίσματα κατὰ τὴν χάριν τὴν δοθεῖσαν ἡμῖν διάφορα,

Rom. 5:15*b*
ἡ δωρεὰ ἐν χάριτι τῇ τοῦ ἑνὸς ἀνθρώπου Ἰησοῦ Χριστοῦ

Rom. 12:4*a*, 5*a*
καθάπερ γὰρ ἐν ἑνὶ σώματι πολλὰ μέλη ἔχομεν, ... οὕτως οἱ πολλοὶ ἓν σῶμά ἐσμεν ἐν Χριστῷ,
Cf. I Cor. 12:4

Cf. I Cor. 12:6

Rom. 9:5*b*
ὁ ὢν ἐπὶ πάντων, θεὸς

Cf. I Cor. 12:7–11
Cf. Rom. 12:3

EPHESIANS 4	COLOSSIAN PARALLELS
9 τὸ δέ "'Ἀνέβη" τί ἐστιν εἰ μὴ ὅτι καὶ κατέβη εἰς τὰ κατώτερα μέρη τῆς γῆς; 10 ὁ καταβὰς αὐτός ἐστιν καὶ ὁ "ἀναβὰς" ὑπεράνω πάντων τῶν οὐρανῶν, ἵνα πληρώσῃ τὰ πάντα. 11 καὶ αὐτὸς "ἔδωκεν" τοὺς μὲν ἀποστόλους, τοὺς δὲ προφήτας, τοὺς δὲ εὐαγγελιστάς,[28] τοὺς δὲ ποιμένας καὶ διδασκάλους,[29] 12 πρὸς τὸν καταρτισμὸν τῶν ἁγίων εἰς ἔργον διακονίας, εἰς οἰκοδομὴν τοῦ σώματος τοῦ χριστοῦ, 13 μέχρι καταντήσωμεν οἱ πάντες	1:19, 20a ὅτι ἐν αὐτῷ εὐδόκησεν πᾶν τὸ πλήρωμα κατοικῆσαι καί δι' αὐτοῦ ἀποκαταλλάξαι τὰ πάντα εἰς αὐτόν,

[28] Acts 21:8b Φιλίππου τοῦ εὐαγγελιστοῦ.
[29] Acts 20:28, ποιμαίνειν τὴν ἐκκλησίαν τοῦ θεοῦ.

Other Pauline Parallels

Rom. 10:6b, 7
"Τίς ἀναβήσεται εἰς τὸν οὐρανόν",
τοῦτ' ἔστιν Χριστὸν καταγαγεῖν·

ἤ "Τίς καταβήσεται εἰς τὴν ἄβυσσον;" τοῦτ' ἔστιν Χριστὸν ἐκ νεκρῶν ἀναγαγεῖν.

II Cor. 12:2b
ἁρπαγέντα τὸν τοιοῦτον ἕως τρίτου οὐρανοῦ.

I Cor. 12:28a
Καὶ οὓς μὲν ἔθετο ὁ θεὸς ἐν τῇ ἐκκλησίᾳ
(Cf. I Cor. 12:5)
πρῶτον ἀποστόλους,
δεύτερον προφήτας,

τρίτον διδασκάλους,

II Cor. 13:9b
τοῦτο καὶ εὐχόμεθα, τὴν ὑμῶν κατάρτισιν.

II Cor. 12:19c
τὰ δὲ πάντα, ἀγαπητοί,
ὑπὲρ τῆς ὑμῶν οἰκοδομῆς,

I Cor. 12:27a
ὑμεῖς δέ ἐστε σῶμα Χριστοῦ

Phil. 3:11
εἴ πως καταντήσω
εἰς τὴν ἐξανάστασιν τὴν ἐκ νεκρῶν.

Rom. 12:6–8b
Ἔχοντες δὲ χαρίσματα κατὰ τὴν χάριν τὴν δοθεῖσαν ἡμῖν

διάφορα,
εἴτε προφητείαν
κατὰ τὴν ἀναλογίαν τῆς πίστεως,
εἴτε διακονίαν ἐν τῇ διακονίᾳ,

εἴτε ὁ διδάσκων ἐν τῇ διδασκαλίᾳ,
εἴτε ὁ παρακαλῶν ἐν τῇ παρακλήσει,

See Rom. 12:7 above

I Cor. 14:26b
πάντα πρὸς οἰκοδομὴν γινέσθω.

EPHESIANS 4	Colossian Parallels
εἰς τὴν ἑνότητα τῆς πίστεως	
καὶ τῆς ἐπιγνώσεως τοῦ υἱοῦ τοῦ θεοῦ,	1:28b ἵνα παραστήσωμεν
εἰς ἄνδρα τέλειον,	πάντα ἄνθρωπον τέλειον ἐν Χριστῷ·
	2:9, 10a
εἰς μέτρον ἡλικίας τοῦ πληρώματος τοῦ χριστοῦ,	ὅτι ἐν αὐτῷ κατοικεῖ πᾶν τὸ πλήρωμα τῆς θεότητος .... καὶ ἐστὲ ἐν αὐτῷ πεπληρωμένοι
	2:8
14 ἵνα μηκέτι ὦμεν νήπιοι,	Βλέπετε μή τις ὑμᾶς ἔσται
κλυδωνιζόμενοι καὶ περιφερόμενοι παντὶ ἀνέμῳ τῆς διδασκαλίας	ὁ συλαγωγῶν διὰ τῆς φιλοσοφίας καὶ κενῆς ἀπάτης
ἐν τῇ κυβίᾳ τῶν ἀνθρώπων	κατὰ τὴν παράδοσιν τῶν ἀνθρώπων,
ἐν πανουργίᾳ πρὸς τὴν μεθοδίαν τῆς πλάνης,	κατὰ τὰ στοιχεῖα τοῦ κόσμου καὶ οὐ κατὰ Χριστόν·
15 ἀληθεύοντες δὲ ἐν ἀγάπῃ	1:10b
αὐξήσωμεν εἰς αὐτὸν τὰ πάντα,	ἐν παντὶ ἔργῳ ἀγαθῷ καρποφοροῦντες καὶ αὐξανόμενοι τῇ ἐπιγνώσει τοῦ θεοῦ,
	1:18a
ὅς ἐστιν ἡ κεφαλή,	καὶ αὐτός ἐστιν ἡ κεφαλὴ τοῦ σώματος, τῆς ἐκκλησίας·
	2:19a
Χριστός,	καὶ οὐ κρατῶν τὴν κεφαλήν,

Other Pauline Parallels

Philem. 6
ὅπως ἡ κοινωνία τῆς πίστεώς σου ἐνεργὴς γένηται
ἐν ἐπιγνώσει παντὸς ἀγαθοῦ
[τοῦ] ἐν ἡμῖν εἰς Χριστόν·

Gal. 2:20b
τοῦ υἱοῦ τοῦ θεοῦ

I Cor. 2:6a
Σοφίαν δὲ λαλοῦμεν ἐν τοῖς τελείοις,

See below

I Cor. 3:1b
ὡς νηπίοις ἐν Χριστῷ.

I Cor. 14:20
Ἀδελφοί, μὴ παιδία γίνεσθε ταῖς φρεσίν, ἀλλὰ τῇ κακίᾳ νηπιάζετε, ταῖς δὲ φρεσὶν τέλειοι γίνεσθε.

Gal. 4:16
ὥστε ἐχθρὸς ὑμῶν γέγονα ἀληθεύων ὑμῖν;

I Cor. 11:3b
παντὸς ἀνδρὸς ἡ κεφαλὴ

ὁ χριστός ἐστιν,

EPHESIANS 4	Colossian Parallels
16 ἐξ οὗ πᾶν τὸ σῶμα See below See below συναρμολογούμενον καὶ συνβιβαζόμενον διὰ πάσης ἁφῆς τῆς ἐπιχορηγίας κατ' ἐνέργειαν ἐν μέτρῳ ἑνὸς ἑκάστου μέρους τὴν αὔξησιν τοῦ σώματος ποιεῖται εἰς οἰκοδομὴν ἑαυτοῦ ἐν ἀγάπῃ.	ἐξ οὗ πᾶν τὸ σῶμα διὰ τῶν ἁφῶν καὶ συνδέσμων ἐπιχορηγούμενον καὶ συνβιβαζόμενον See above 1:29b ἀγωνιζόμενος κατὰ τὴν ἐνέργειαν αὐτοῦ 2:19b αὔξει τὴν αὔξησιν τοῦ θεοῦ. 2:4a; cf. 2:6 below
17 Τοῦτο οὖν λέγω καὶ μαρτύρομαι ἐν κυρίῳ, μηκέτι ὑμᾶς περιπατεῖν καθὼς καὶ τὰ ἔθνη περιπατεῖ ἐν ματαιότητι τοῦ νοὸς αὐτῶν,	Τοῦτο λέγω 3:7 ἐν οἷς καὶ ὑμεῖς περιεπατήσατέ ποτε ὅτε ἐζῆτε ἐν τούτοις·
18 ἐσκοτωμένοι τῇ διανοίᾳ ὄντες, ἀπηλλοτριωμένοι τῆς ζωῆς τοῦ θεοῦ, διὰ τὴν ἄγνοιαν τὴν οὖσαν ἐν αὐτοῖς, διὰ τὴν πώρωσιν τῆς καρδίας αὐτῶν,	1:21a καὶ ὑμᾶς ποτὲ ὄντας ἀπηλλο- τριωμένους

Other Pauline Parallels

Phil. 3:21 κατὰ τὴν ἐνέργειαν	II Thess. 2:9b κατ' ἐνέργειαν τοῦ Σατανᾶ
I Cor. 14:12b πρὸς τὴν οἰκοδομὴν τῆς ἐκκλησίας	II Cor. 10:8b; 13:10b εἰς οἰκοδομὴν
Cf. Rom. 1:18–32	
Gal. 5:3a μαρτύρομαι δὲ πάλιν	
Rom. 8:20a τῇ γὰρ ματαιότητι ἡ κτίσις ὑπετάγη,	
Rom. 1:21b ἀλλὰ ἐματαιώθησαν ἐν τοῖς διαλογισμοῖς αὐτῶν καὶ ἐσκοτίσθη ἡ ἀσύνετος αὐτῶν καρδία·	
Rom. 10:3a ἀγνοοῦντες γὰρ τὴν τοῦ θεοῦ δικαιοσύνην,	
Rom. 11:25b πώρωσις ἀπὸ μέρους τῷ Ἰσραὴλ γέγονεν	

EPHESIANS 4	Colossian Parallels
19 οἵτινες ἀπηλγηκότες ἑαυτοὺς παρέδωκαν τῇ ἀσελγείᾳ	
	3:5b
εἰς ἐργασίαν ἀκαθαρσίας πάσης	ἀκαθαρσίαν, ...
ἐν πλεονεξίᾳ.	καὶ τὴν πλεονεξίαν . . . .
	2:6, 7
20 Ὑμεῖς δὲ οὐχ οὕτως ἐμάθετε τὸν χριστόν,	Ὡς οὖν παρελάβετε τὸν χριστὸν Ἰησοῦν τὸν κύριον,
21 εἴ γε αὐτὸν ἠκούσατε καὶ ἐν αὐτῷ ἐδιδάχθητε,	ἐν αὐτῷ περιπατεῖτε, ... καθὼς ἐδιδάχθητε,
καθώς ἐστιν ἀλήθεια ἐν τῷ Ἰησοῦ,	
	3:8a, 9
22 ἀποθέσθαι ὑμᾶς	νυνὶ δὲ ἀπόθεσθε καὶ ὑμεῖς τὰ πάντα, ...
See 24a below κατὰ τὴν προτέραν ἀναστροφὴν	
τὸν παλαιὸν ἄνθρωπον τὸν φθειρόμενον	ἀπεκδυσάμενοι τὸν παλαιὸν ἄνθρωπον
κατὰ τὰς ἐπιθυμίας τῆς ἀπάτης,	σὺν ταῖς πράξεσιν αὐτοῦ,
23 ἀνανεοῦσθαι δὲ	See below
	2:18b
τῷ πνεύματι τοῦ νοὸς ὑμῶν,	ὑπὸ τοῦ νοὸς τῆς σαρκὸς αὐτοῦ
	3:10
24 καὶ ἐνδύσασθαι τὸν καινὸν ἄνθρωπον	καὶ ἐνδυσάμενοι τὸν νέον τὸν ἀνακαινούμενον εἰς ἐπίγνωσιν
τὸν κατὰ θεὸν κτισθέντα	"κατ' εἰκόνα τοῦ κτίσαντος" αὐτόν,
ἐν δικαιοσύνῃ καὶ ὁσιότητι τῆς ἀληθείας.[30]	

[30] Luke 1:75a, λατρεύειν αὐτῷ ἐν ὁσιότητι καὶ δικαιοσύνῃ.

Other Pauline Parallels

Rom. 1:24
Διὸ παρέδωκεν αὐτοὺς ὁ θεὸς ἐν ταῖς ἐπιθυμίαις τῶν καρδιῶν αὐτῶν
εἰς ἀκαθαρσίαν

See below

II Cor. 12:21b
ἐπὶ τῇ ἀκαθαρσίᾳ καὶ πορνείᾳ καὶ ἀσελγείᾳ ᾗ ἔπραξαν.

II Cor. 11:10a
ἔστιν ἀλήθεια Χριστοῦ ἐν ἐμοὶ
Rom. 9:1a
Ἀλήθειαν λέγω ἐν Χριστῷ,
Cf. Rom. 8:13; Gal. 6:8

Cf. Gal. 1:13a
τὴν ἐμὴν ἀναστροφήν ποτε
Rom. 6:6
ὁ παλαιὸς ἡμῶν ἄνθρωπος
Rom. 6:12b
εἰς τὸ ὑπακούειν ταῖς ἐπιθυμίαις αὐτοῦ,
Rom. 12:2b
μεταμορφοῦσθε τῇ ἀνακαινώσει τοῦ νοός
Gal. 3:27b
Χριστὸν ἐνεδύσασθε·

Rom. 13:12b
ἀποθώμεθα οὖν τὰ ἔργα τοῦ σκότους,
ἐνδυσώμεθα [δὲ] τὰ ὅπλα τοῦ φωτός.

II Cor. 11:3a
φοβοῦμαι δὲ μή πως, ὡς "ὁ ὄφις ἐξηπάτησεν" Εὕαν . . . .
φθαρῇ τὰ νοήματα ὑμῶν

Rom. 13:14a, cf. 12b
ἀλλὰ ἐνδύσασθε τὸν κύριον Ἰησοῦν Χριστόν,
Rom. 6:4b
οὕτως καὶ ἡμεῖς ἐν καινότητι ζωῆς περιπατήσωμεν.

EPHESIANS 4	COLOSSIAN PARALLELS
25 Διὸ ἀποθέμενοι	3:8a νυνὶ δὲ ἀπόθεσθε καὶ ὑμεῖς τὰ πάντα,
τὸ ψεῦδος "λαλεῖτε ἀλήθειαν"[31] "ἕκαστος μετὰ τοῦ πλησίον αὐτοῦ," ὅτι ἐσμὲν ἀλλήλων μέλη.	3:9a μὴ ψεύδεσθε εἰς ἀλλήλους·
26 "ὀργίζεσθε καὶ μὴ ἁμαρτάνετε·"[32] ὁ ἥλιος μὴ ἐπιδυέτω ἐπὶ παροργισμῷ ὑμῶν,	3:8b ὀργήν, θυμόν,
27 μηδὲ δίδοτε τόπον τῷ διαβόλῳ.[33]	
28 ὁ κλέπτων μηκέτι κλεπτέτω, μᾶλλον δὲ κοπιάτω ἐργαζόμενος ταῖς χερσὶν τὸ ἀγαθόν,	

[31] Zech. 8:16b, λαλεῖτε ἀλήθειαν ἕκαστος πρὸς τὸν πλησίον αὐτοῦ.
[32] Ps. 4:5a, ὀργίζεσθε καὶ μὴ ἁμαρτάνετε·
[33] Cf. Acts 13:10b, υἱὲ διαβόλου.

Other Pauline Parallels

Rom. 13:12b
ἀποθώμεθα οὖν τὰ ἔργα τοῦ σκότους,

Rom. 12:5b
ἓν σῶμά ἐσμεν ἐν Χριστῷ, τὸ δὲ καθ' εἷς ἀλλήλων μέλη.

I Cor. 15:34a
ἐκνήψατε δικαίως καὶ μὴ ἁμαρτάνετε,

See below

Rom. 12:19b
ἀλλὰ δότε τόπον τῇ ὀργῇ,

II Cor. 2:11
ἵνα μὴ πλεονεκτηθῶμεν ὑπὸ τοῦ Σατανᾶ, οὐ γὰρ αὐτοῦ τὰ νοήματα ἀγνοοῦμεν.

Rom. 2:21b
ὁ κηρύσσων μὴ κλέπτειν κλέπτεις;

I Cor. 4:12a
καὶ κοπιῶμεν

I Thess. 4:11b, 12b
ἐργαζόμενοι   ἐργάζεσθαι

ταῖς ἰδίαις χερ- ταῖς χερσὶν ὑμῶν,
σὶν·

Rom. 2:10b   Gal. 6:10b
παντὶ τῷ ἐργα-   ἐργαζώμεθα
ζομένῳ

τὸ ἀγαθόν,   τὸ ἀγαθὸν πρὸς
                 πάντας,

EPHESIANS 4	Colossian Parallels
ἵνα ἔχῃ μεταδιδόναι τῷ χρείαν ἔχοντι.	
	3:8 νυνὶ δὲ ἀπόθεσθε καὶ ὑμεῖς .... βλασφημίαν, αἰσχρολογίαν ἐκ τοῦ στόματος ὑμῶν· (cf. 4:6 below)
29 πᾶς λόγος σαπρὸς ἐκ τοῦ στόματος ὑμῶν μὴ ἐκπορευέσθω,	
	3:16a, c ὁ λόγος τοῦ χριστοῦ ἐνοικείτω
ἀλλὰ εἴ τις ἀγαθὸς	
πρὸς οἰκοδομὴν τῆς χρείας,	διδάσκοντες καὶ νουθετοῦντες ἑαυτοὺς
	4:6a ὁ λόγος ὑμῶν πάντοτε ἐν χάριτι, ἅλατι ἠρτυμένος,
ἵνα δῷ χάριν τοῖς ἀκούουσιν. 30 καὶ μὴ λυπεῖτε	
τὸ πνεῦμα τὸ ἅγιον τοῦ θεοῦ,[34]	
ἐν ᾧ ἐσφραγίσθητε	
εἰς ἡμέραν ἀπολυτρώσεως.[35]	3:8 νυνὶ δὲ ἀπόθεσθε καὶ ὑμεῖς τὰ πάντα,
31 πᾶσα πικρία καὶ θυμὸς καὶ ὀργὴ καὶ κραυγὴ καὶ βλασφημία ἀρθήτω ἀφ' ὑμῶν σὺν πάσῃ κακίᾳ.	ὀργήν, θυμόν, κακίαν, βλασφημίαν, αἰσχρολογίαν ἐκ τοῦ στόματος ὑμῶν· See above

[34] Isa. 63:10b, καὶ παρώξυναν τὸ πνεῦμα τὸ ἅγιον αὐτοῦ.
[35] Isa. 49:8b, ἐν ἡμέρᾳ σωτηρίας ἐβοήθησά σοι.

Other Pauline Parallels

．．．．ἵνα．．．．

Rom. 12:13a
ταῖς χρείαις τῶν ἁγίων κοινωνοῦντες,

μηδενὸς χρείαν ἔχητε.

II Thess. 2:17b
ἐν παντὶ ἔργῳ καὶ λόγῳ ἀγαθῷ.
I Cor. 14:26b
πάντα πρὸς οἰκοδομὴν γινέσθω.

I Thess. 5:19
τὸ πνεῦμα μὴ σβέννυτε,
I Thess. 4:8b
τὸν θεὸν τὸν "διδόντα τὸ πνεῦμα αὐτοῦ" τὸ ἅγιον "εἰς ὑμᾶς."
II Cor. 1:22
[ὁ] καὶ σφραγισάμενος ἡμᾶς καὶ δοὺς τὸν ἀρραβῶνα τοῦ πνεύματος ἐν ταῖς καρδίαις ἡμῶν.
II Cor. 6:2b
"ἐν ἡμέρᾳ σωτηρίας"

Rom. 8:23a, c, cf. 18–23
τὴν ἀπαρχὴν τοῦ πνεύματος ἔχοντες ....

υἱοθεσίαν ἀπεκδεχόμενοι

τὴν ἀπολύτρωσιν τοῦ σώματος ἡμῶν.

I Cor. 5:2b
ἵνα ἀρθῇ ἐκ μέσου ὑμῶν

EPHESIANS 4	COLOSSIAN PARALLELS
	3:12, 13
32 γίνεσθε[δὲ]εἰς ἀλλήλους χρηστοί, εὔσπλαγχνοι,	Ἐνδύσασθε οὖν . . . . σπλάγχνα οἰκτιρμοῦ, χρηστότητα, ...
χαριζόμενοι ἑαυτοῖς καθὼς καὶ ὁ θεὸς ἐν Χριστῷ ἐχαρίσατο ὑμῖν.	καὶ χαριζόμενοι ἑαυτοῖς . . . . καθὼς καὶ ὁ κύριος ἐχαρίσατο ὑμῖν οὕτως καὶ ὑμεῖς·
5	3:12a
1 γίνεσθε οὖν μιμηταὶ τοῦ θεοῦ,	Ἐνδύσασθε οὖν ὡς ἐκλεκτοὶ τοῦ θεοῦ,
ὡς τέκνα ἀγαπητά,	ἅγιοι καὶ ἠγαπημένοι,
2 καὶ περιπατεῖτε ἐν ἀγάπῃ,	
καθὼς καὶ ὁ χριστὸς ἠγάπησεν ὑμᾶς καὶ παρέδωκεν ἑαυτὸν ὑπὲρ ὑμῶν	
"προσφορὰν καὶ θυσίαν" τῷ θεῷ[36] "εἰς ὀσμὴν εὐωδίας."[37]	3:5a
	Νεκρώσατε οὖν τὰ μέλη τὰ ἐπὶ τῆς γῆς,
3 Πορνεία δὲ καὶ ἀκαθαρσία πᾶσα ἢ πλεονεξία	πορνείαν, ἀκαθαρσίαν, πάθος, ἐπιθυμίαν κακήν, καὶ τὴν πλεονεξίαν
μηδὲ ὀνομαζέσθω ἐν ὑμῖν,	
καθὼς πρέπει ἁγίοις,	3:8
4 καὶ αἰσχρότης καὶ μωρολογία	ἀπόθεσθε . . . . αἰσχρολογίαν ἐκ τοῦ στόματος ὑμῶν

[36] Ps. 39 (40):7a, θυσίαν καὶ προσφοράν.
[37] Ezek. 20:41a, ἐν ὀσμῇ εὐωδίας.

Other Pauline Parallels

I Cor. 4:16b
μιμηταί μου γίνεσθε.

I Cor. 4:14b
ὡς τέκνα μου ἀγαπητὰ νουθετῶν·

Rom. 14:15b
οὐκέτι κατὰ ἀγάπην περιπατεῖς.

Gal. 2:20b
τοῦ υἱοῦ τοῦ θεοῦ τοῦ ἀγαπήσαντός με
καὶ παραδόντος ἑαυτὸν ὑπὲρ ἐμοῦ.

Phil. 4:18b
"ὀσμὴν εὐωδίας,"
θυσίαν δεκτήν, εὐάρεστον τῷ θεῷ.
See above

II Cor. 12:21b; cf. Rom. 1: 24–32
ἐπὶ τῇ ἀκαθαρσίᾳ καὶ πορνείᾳ

καὶ ἀσελγείᾳ

I Cor. 5:11b
ἐάν τις ἀδελφὸς ὀνομαζόμενος ᾖ πόρνος ἢ πλεονέκτης ἢ εἰδωλολάτρης

I Cor. 11:1
μιμηταί μου γίνεσθε, καθὼς κἀγὼ Χριστοῦ.

EPHESIANS 5	Colossian Parallels
ἢ εὐτραπελία,	
ἃ οὐκ ἀνῆκεν,	
	2:7b
ἀλλὰ μᾶλλον εὐχαριστία.[38]	περισσεύοντες [ἐν αὐτῇ] ἐν εὐχαριστίᾳ.
	3:15b
5 τοῦτο γὰρ ἴστε γινώσκοντες	καὶ εὐχάριστοι γίνεσθε.
	3:5b
ὅτι πᾶς πόρνος ἢ ἀκάθαρτος	πορνείαν, ἀκαθαρσίαν, ...
ἢ πλεονέκτης,	καὶ τὴν πλεονεξίαν
ὅ ἐστιν εἰδωλολάτρης,	ἥτις ἐστὶν εἰδωλολατρία,
οὐκ ἔχει κληρονομίαν ἐν τῇ βασιλείᾳ	
τοῦ χριστοῦ καὶ θεοῦ.	
	2:4b
6 Μηδεὶς ὑμᾶς ἀπατάτω	ἵνα μηδεὶς ὑμᾶς παραλογίζηται
κενοῖς λόγοις,[39]	ἐν πιθανολογίᾳ.
	3:6
διὰ ταῦτα γὰρ ἔρχεται ἡ ὀργὴ τοῦ θεοῦ	δι' ἃ ἔρχεται ἡ ὀργὴ τοῦ θεοῦ·
ἐπὶ τοὺς υἱοὺς τῆς ἀπειθίας.	

[38] 3:17b, εὐχαριστοῦντες τῷ θεῷ πατρὶ δι' αὐτοῦ.

[39] 2:8a, Βλέπετε μή τις ὑμᾶς ἔσται ὁ συλαγωγῶν διὰ τῆς φιλοσοφίας καὶ κενῆς ἀπάτης.

Other Pauline Parallels

Rom. 1:28b ποιεῖν τὰ μὴ καθήκοντα, I Thess. 5:18 ἐν παντὶ εὐχαριστεῖτε·	
I Cor. 6:9a ἢ οὐκ οἴδατε	I Cor. 6:9b, 10b Μὴ πλανᾶσθε·

ὅτι ἄδικοι	Gal. 5:19–21
	οὔτε πόρνοι ἅτινά ἐστιν
	               πορνεία, ἀκα-
	               θαρσία, ἀσέλ-
	               γεια,
	οὔτε εἰδωλολά- εἰδωλολατρία,
	τραι οὔτε μοιχοὶ . . . .
	. . . .
	οὔτε πλεονέκ- οἱ τὰ τοιαῦτα
	ται, ... πράσσοντες

θεοῦ βασιλείαν οὐ κληρονομήσουσιν;	βασιλείαν θεοῦ βασιλείαν θεοῦ κληρονομήσου- οὐ κληρονομή- σιν. σουσιν.
See above	
Rom. 1:18a Ἀποκαλύπτεται γὰρ ὀργὴ θεοῦ ἀπ' οὐρανοῦ ἐπὶ πᾶσαν ἀσέβειαν καὶ ἀδικίαν ἀνθρώπων	

EPHESIANS 5	Colossian Parallels
7 μὴ οὖν γίνεσθε συνμέτοχοι αὐτῶν·	
8 ἦτε γάρ ποτε σκότος,	
νῦν δὲ φῶς ἐν κυρίῳ·	
ὡς τέκνα φωτὸς περιπατεῖτε,	Cf. 1:12
9 ὁ γὰρ καρπὸς τοῦ φωτὸς	
ἐν πάσῃ ἀγαθωσύνῃ	
καὶ δικαιοσύνῃ καὶ ἀληθείᾳ,	
10 δοκιμάζοντες τί ἐστιν εὐάρεστον τῷ κυρίῳ·	3:20b τοῦτο γὰρ εὐάρεστόν ἐστιν ἐν κυρίῳ.
11 καὶ μὴ συνκοινωνεῖτε	
τοῖς ἔργοις τοῖς ἀκάρποις τοῦ σκότους,	
μᾶλλον δὲ καὶ ἐλέγχετε,	
12 τὰ γὰρ κρυφῇ γινόμενα ὑπ' αὐτῶν αἰσχρόν ἐστιν καὶ λέγειν·	3:8a νυνὶ δὲ ἀπόθεσθε .... τὰ πάντα, ... αἰσχρολογίαν
13 τὰ δὲ πάντα ἐλεγχόμενα ὑπὸ τοῦ φωτὸς[40]	

[40] Cf. Luke 11:34-36.

EPHESIANS AND THE PAULINE LETTERS 143

Other Pauline Parallels

II Cor. 6:14
Μὴ γίνεσθε ἑτεροζυγοῦντες ἀπίστοις· τίς γὰρ μετοχὴ δικαιοσύνῃ καὶ ἀνομίᾳ, ἢ τίς κοινωνία φωτὶ πρὸς σκότος;

Rom. 2:19b; cf. I Cor. 6:14
φῶς τῶν ἐν σκότει,

I Thess. 5:5; cf. Rom. 13:12
πάντες γὰρ ὑμεῖς
υἱοὶ φωτός ἐστε καὶ υἱοὶ ἡμέρας.

Gal. 5:22, 23a
ὁ δὲ καρπὸς τοῦ πνεύματός ἐστιν ἀγάπη, χαρά, εἰρήνη, μακροθυμία, χρηστότης, ἀγαθωσύνη,
πίστις, πραΰτης, ἐγκράτεια·

Rom. 12:2b
εἰς τὸ δοκιμάζειν ὑμᾶς τί τὸ θέλημα τοῦ θεοῦ, τὸ ἀγαθὸν καὶ εὐάρεστον καὶ τέλειον.

II Cor. 6:14b
ἢ τίς κοινωνία φωτὶ πρὸς σκότος;

Rom. 13:12b
ἀποθώμεθα οὖν τὰ ἔργα τοῦ σκότους,

Cf. Rom. 1:24, 26, 27

Cf. I Cor. 11:6; 14:35 (αἰσχρόν)

I Cor. 14:24b, 25a
ἐλέγχεται ὑπὸ πάντων, ἀνακρίνεται ὑπὸ πάντων,

Rom. 13:12b, 13a
ἀποθώμεθα οὖν τὰ ἔργα τοῦ σκότους,
ἐνδυσώμεθα [δὲ] τὰ ὅπλα τοῦ φωτός.

ὡς ἐν ἡμέρᾳ εὐσχημόνως περιπατήσωμεν,

Phil. 4:18b
εὐάρεστον τῷ θεῷ.

I Cor. 4:5b
ὃς καὶ φωτίσει τὰ κρυπτὰ τοῦ σκότους

EPHESIANS 5	COLOSSIAN PARALLELS
φανεροῦται,	
πᾶν γὰρ τὸ φανερούμενον φῶς ἐστίν.	
14 διὸ λέγει Ἔγειρε, ὁ καθεύδων, καὶ ἀνάστα ἐκ τῶν νεκρῶν, καὶ ἐπιφαύσει σοι ὁ χριστός.	
15 Βλέπετε οὖν ἀκριβῶς πῶς	
	4:5 Ἐν σοφίᾳ
περιπατεῖτε,	περιπατεῖτε πρὸς τοὺς ἔξω,
μὴ ὡς ἄσοφοι	
ἀλλ' ὡς σοφοί,	
16 ἐξαγοραζόμενοι τὸν καιρόν,	τὸν καιρὸν ἐξαγοραζόμενοι.
ὅτι αἱ ἡμέραι πονηραί εἰσιν.	
17 διὰ τοῦτο	Cf. 1:9
μὴ γίνεσθε ἄφρονες,	
	4:12b
ἀλλὰ συνίετε τί τὸ θέλημα τοῦ κυρίου·	καὶ πεπληροφορημένοι ἐν παντὶ θελήματι τοῦ θεοῦ.
18 καὶ "μὴ μεθύσκεσθε οἴνῳ,"[41]	

[41] Prov. 23:31, μὴ μεθύσκεσθε ἐν οἴνοις.

Other Pauline Parallels

τὰ κρυπτὰ τῆς καρδίας αὐτοῦ φανερὰ γίνεται,	καὶ φανερώσει τὰς βουλὰς τῶν καρδιῶν,
I Cor. 3:10b ἕκαστος δὲ βλεπέτω πῶς ἐποικοδομεῖ·	Βλέπετε (ten times in the Pauline letters)
Rom. 13:13a ὡς ἐν ἡμέρᾳ εὐσχημόνως περιπατήσωμεν,	
Rom. 16:19b θέλω δὲ ὑμᾶς σοφοὺς [μὲν] εἶναι εἰς τὸ ἀγαθόν,	
Gal. 1:4b ὅπως ἐξέληται ἡμᾶς ἐκ τοῦ αἰῶνος τοῦ ἐνεστῶτος πονηροῦ Cf. Rom. 1:26; I Cor. 4:17, etc. Cf. II Cor. 12:11a Γέγονα ἄφρων· Gal. 3:3a οὕτως ἀνόητοί ἐστε;	
Rom. 2:17b, 18a καυχᾶσαι ἐν θεῷ καὶ γινώσκεις τὸ θέλημα	Rom. 12:2b εἰς τὸ δοκιμάζειν ὑμᾶς τί τὸ θέλημα τοῦ θεοῦ,
Cf. Rom. 13:13b μὴ κώμοις καὶ μέθαις,	I Thess. 5:7b καὶ οἱ μεθυσκόμενοι νυκτὸς μεθύουσιν.

EPHESIANS 5	Colossian Parallels
ἐν ᾧ ἐστὶν ἀσωτία,[42]	
ἀλλὰ πληροῦσθε ἐν πνεύματι,[43]	3:16b, 17
19 λαλοῦντες ἑαυτοῖς	διδάσκοντες καὶ νουθετοῦντες
ψαλμοῖς καὶ ὕμνοις	ἑαυτοὺς
	ψαλμοῖς, ὕμνοις,
καὶ ᾠδαῖς πνευματικαῖς,	ᾠδαῖς πνευματικαῖς ἐν χάριτι,
ᾄδοντες καὶ ψάλλοντες	ᾄδοντες
τῇ καρδίᾳ ὑμῶν	ἐν ταῖς καρδίαις ὑμῶν
τῷ κυρίῳ,	τῷ θεῷ·
20 εὐχαριστοῦντες	See below
πάντοτε ὑπὲρ πάντων	καὶ πᾶν ὅτι ἐὰν ποιῆτε ἐν λόγῳ ἢ
	ἐν ἔργῳ, πάντα
ἐν ὀνόματι τοῦ κυρίου ἡμῶν Ἰησοῦ Χριστοῦ	ἐν ὀνόματι κυρίου Ἰησοῦ,
	εὐχαριστοῦντες
τῷ θεῷ καὶ πατρί,	τῷ θεῷ πατρὶ δι' αὐτοῦ.
21 ὑποτασσόμενοι ἀλλήλοις[44]	
ἐν φόβῳ Χριστοῦ.	3:18
22 Αἱ γυναῖκες τοῖς ἰδίοις ἀνδράσιν	Αἱ γυναῖκες, ὑποτάσσεσθε τοῖς ἀνδράσιν,
ὡς τῷ κυρίῳ,	ὡς ἀνῆκεν ἐν κυρίῳ.
23 ὅτι ἀνήρ ἐστιν κεφαλὴ τῆς γυναικὸς	1:18
ὡς καὶ ὁ χριστὸς κεφαλὴ	καὶ αὐτός ἐστιν ἡ κεφαλὴ
τῆς ἐκκλησίας,	τοῦ σώματος,
αὐτὸς σωτὴρ τοῦ σώματος.	τῆς ἐκκλησίας·
24 ἀλλὰ ὡς ἡ ἐκκλησία ὑποτάσσεται τῷ χριστῷ,	
οὕτως καὶ αἱ γυναῖκες τοῖς ἀνδράσιν ἐν παντί.	Cf. 3:18 above

[42] Cf. Luke 15:13, ζῶν ἀσώτως.
[43] Cf. Luke 4:1; Acts 7:55, etc., πλήρης πνεύματος ἁγίου.

Other Pauline Parallels

I Cor. 14:15b
ψαλῶ τῷ πνεύματι,
ψαλῶ [δὲ] καὶ τῷ νοΐ·

I Thess. 5:18a
ἐν παντὶ εὐχαριστεῖτε·

Phil. 1:3, 4
Εὐχαριστῶ τῷ θεῷ μου . . . .
πάντοτε . . . . ὑπὲρ πάντων ὑμῶν,

Gal. 5:13b
ἀλλὰ διὰ τῆς ἀγάπης δουλεύετε
ἀλλήλοις·

Phil. 2:3b
ἀλλήλους ἡγούμενοι ὑπερέχοντας
ἑαυτῶν, (cf. II Cor. 5:11; 7:1)

I Cor. 11:3b; cf. 14:34
παντὸς ἀνδρὸς ἡ κεφαλὴ ὁ χριστός ἐστιν,
κεφαλὴ δὲ γυναικὸς ὁ ἀνήρ,

See above

Phil. 3:20b
ἐξ οὗ καὶ σωτῆρα ἀπεκδεχόμεθα
κύριον Ἰησοῦν Χριστόν,

[44] Rom. 12:10b, τῇ τιμῇ ἀλλήλους προηγούμενοι.

EPHESIANS 5	Colossian Parallels
	3:19
25 Οἱ ἄνδρες, ἀγαπᾶτε τὰς γυναῖκας,	Οἱ ἄνδρες, ἀγαπᾶτε τὰς γυναῖκας
	καὶ μὴ πικραίνεσθε πρὸς αὐτάς.
καθὼς καὶ ὁ χριστὸς ἠγάπησεν τὴν ἐκκλησίαν καὶ ἑαυτὸν παρέδωκεν ὑπὲρ αὐτῆς,	
26 ἵνα αὐτὴν ἁγιάσῃ	
καθαρίσας τῷ λουτρῷ τοῦ ὕδατος	
ἐν ῥήματι,	
	1:22b
27 ἵνα παραστήσῃ αὐτὸς ἑαυτῷ ἔνδοξον τὴν ἐκκλησίαν, μὴ ἔχουσαν σπίλον ἢ ῥυτίδα	παραστῆσαι ὑμᾶς
ἤ τι τῶν τοιούτων,	
ἀλλ' ἵνα ᾖ ἁγία καὶ ἄμωμος.	ἁγίους καὶ ἀμώμους καὶ ἀνεγκλήτους κατενώπιον αὐτοῦ,
	3:19a
28 οὕτως ὀφείλουσιν [καὶ] οἱ ἄνδρες	Οἱ ἄνδρες,
ἀγαπᾶν τὰς ἑαυτῶν γυναῖκας	ἀγαπᾶτε τὰς γυναῖκας
ὡς τὰ ἑαυτῶν σώματα· ὁ ἀγαπῶν τὴν ἑαυτοῦ γυναῖκα ἑαυτὸν ἀγαπᾷ,	
29 οὐδεὶς γάρ ποτε τὴν ἑαυτοῦ σάρκα ἐμίσησεν,	

OTHER PAULINE PARALLELS

Gal. 2:20b
τοῦ υἱοῦ τοῦ θεοῦ τοῦ ἀγαπήσαντός με
καὶ παραδόντος ἑαυτὸν ὑπὲρ ἐμοῦ.
See below; cf. II Cor. 7:1b

I Cor. 6:11b
ἀλλὰ ἀπελούσασθε, ἀλλὰ ἡγιάσθητε,

Rom. 10:9a
ὅτι ἐὰν ὁμολογήσῃς "τὸ ῥῆμα ἐν τῷ στόματί σου"
ὅτι ΚΥΡΙΟΣ ΙΗΣΟΥΣ,

II Cor. 11:2b
ἡρμοσάμην γὰρ ὑμᾶς ἑνὶ ἀνδρὶ

παρθένον ἁγνὴν

παραστῆσαι τῷ χριστῷ·

Cf. I Cor. 7:3, 4
τῇ γυναικὶ ὁ ἀνὴρ τὴν ὀφειλὴν ἀποδιδότω, ὁμοίως δὲ καὶ ἡ γυνὴ τῷ ἀνδρί.
ἡ γυνὴ τοῦ ἰδίου σώματος οὐκ ἐξουσιάζει
ἀλλὰ ὁ ἀνήρ· ὁμοίως δὲ καὶ
ὁ ἀνὴρ τοῦ ἰδίου σώματος οὐκ ἐξουσιάζει ἀλλὰ ἡ γυνή.
Cf. I Cor. 6:16 below

EPHESIANS 5	COLOSSIAN PARALLELS
ἀλλὰ ἐκτρέφει καὶ θάλπει αὐτήν,	
καθὼς καὶ ὁ χριστὸς τὴν ἐκκλησίαν,	
30 ὅτι μέλη ἐσμὲν τοῦ σώματος αὐτοῦ.	
31 "ἀντὶ τούτου καταλείψει ἄνθρωπος" "[τὸν] πατέρα καὶ [τὴν] μητέρα" "καὶ προσκολληθήσεται πρὸς τὴν γυναῖκα αὐτοῦ," "καὶ ἔσονται οἱ δύο εἰς σάρκα μίαν."[45]	
32 τὸ μυστήριον τοῦτο μέγα ἐστίν,	
ἐγὼ δὲ λέγω εἰς Χριστὸν καὶ [εἰς] τὴν ἐκκλησίαν.	
33 πλὴν καὶ ὑμεῖς οἱ καθ' ἕνα	
ἕκαστος τὴν ἑαυτοῦ γυναῖκα	
οὕτως ἀγαπάτω ὡς ἑαυτόν,	
	3:18a, 20, 21
ἡ δὲ γυνὴ ἵνα φοβῆται τὸν ἄνδρα.	Αἱ γυναῖκες, ὑποτάσσεσθε τοῖς ἀνδράσιν, ...

[45] Gen. 2:24, ἕνεκεν τούτου καταλείψει ἄνθρωπος τὸν πατέρα αὐτοῦ καὶ τὴν μητέρα αὐτοῦ, καὶ προσκολληθήσεται τῇ γυναικὶ αὐτοῦ· καὶ ἔσονται οἱ δύο εἰς σάρκα μίαν.

Other Pauline Parallels

I Thess. 2:7b
ὡς ἐὰν τροφὸς θάλπῃ τὰ ἑαυτῆς τέκνα·

I Cor. 6:15a
οὐκ οἴδατε ὅτι τὰ σώματα ὑμῶν μέλη Χριστοῦ ἐστίν;

Rom. 12:5
οὕτως οἱ πολλοὶ ἓν σῶμά ἐσμεν ἐν Χριστῷ, τὸ δὲ καθ' εἷς ἀλλήλων μέλη.

I Cor. 6:16b
'"Ἔσονται" γάρ, φησίν, "οἱ δύο εἰς σάρκα μίαν."

Rom. 11:25a
Οὐ γὰρ θέλω ὑμᾶς ἀγνοεῖν, ... τὸ μυστήριον τοῦτο,

I Cor. 15:51a
ἰδοὺ μυστήριον ὑμῖν λέγω·

I Cor. 11:11a
πλὴν οὔτε γυνὴ χωρὶς ἀνδρὸς

I Cor. 7:2b
ἕκαστος τὴν ἑαυτοῦ γυναῖκα ἐχέτω,

Rom. 13:9b; Gal. 5:14b
'"Ἀγαπήσεις τὸν πλησίον σου ὡς σεαυτόν."

Cf. I Cor. 11:3b
κεφαλὴ δὲ γυναικὸς ὁ ἀνήρ,

Rom. 12:5b
καθ' εἷς

EPHESIANS 6	COLOSSIAN PARALLELS
6	
1 Τὰ τέκνα, ὑπακούετε τοῖς γονεῦσιν ὑμῶν [ἐν κυρίῳ], τοῦτο γάρ ἐστιν δίκαιον·	Τὰ τέκνα, ὑπακούετε τοῖς γονεῦσιν κατὰ πάντα, See below τοῦτο γὰρ εὐάρεστόν ἐστιν ἐν κυρίῳ.
2 "τίμα τὸν πατέρα σου καὶ τὴν μητέρα," ἥτις ἐστὶν ἐντολὴ πρώτη ἐν ἐπαγγελίᾳ,	
3 "ἵνα εὖ σοι γένηται" "καὶ ἔσῃ μακροχρόνιος ἐπὶ τῆς γῆς."[46]	
4 Καὶ οἱ πατέρες, μὴ παροργίζετε τὰ τέκνα ὑμῶν, ἀλλὰ ἐκτρέφετε αὐτὰ ἐν "παιδείᾳ" καὶ "νουθεσίᾳ Κυρίου."[47]	Οἱ πατέρες, μὴ ἐρεθίζετε τὰ τέκνα ὑμῶν, ἵνα μὴ ἀθυμῶσιν. Cf. 3:16c
5 Οἱ δοῦλοι, ὑπακούετε τοῖς κατὰ σάρκα κυρίοις μετὰ φόβου καὶ τρόμου ἐν ἁπλότητι τῆς καρδίας ὑμῶν ὡς τῷ χριστῷ,	3:22a Οἱ δοῦλοι, ὑπακούετε κατὰ πάντα τοῖς κατὰ σάρκα κυρίοις, See below 3:23b ὡς τῷ κυρίῳ

[46] Exod. 20:12a, Τίμα τὸν πατέρα σου καὶ τὴν μητέρα, ἵνα εὖ σοι γένηται, καὶ ἵνα μακροχρόνιος γένῃ ἐπὶ τῆς γῆς.

[47] Isa. 50:5a, ἡ παιδία κυρίου Κυρίου. Prov. 2:2b, παραβαλεῖς δὲ αὐτὴν ἐπὶ νουθέτησιν τῷ υἱῷ σου.

Other Pauline Parallels

I Cor. 4:14b
ὡς τέκνα μου ἀγαπητά

νουθετῶν

Phil. 2:12b, c
καθὼς πάντοτε ὑπηκούσατε, ...

Rom. 6:16b
δοῦλοί ἐστε
ᾧ ὑπακούετε,

II Cor. 7:15b; cf. I Cor. 2:3
μετὰ φόβου καὶ τρόμου

μετὰ φόβου καὶ τρόμου . . . .

EPHESIANS 6	COLOSSIAN PARALLELS
	3:22b
6 μὴ κατ' ὀφθαλμοδουλίαν ὡς ἀνθρωπάρεσκοι	μὴ ἐν ὀφθαλμοδουλίαις, ὡς ἀνθρωπάρεσκοι,
ἀλλ'	ἀλλ' ἐν ἁπλότητι καρδίας,
	3:24b
ὡς δοῦλοι Χριστοῦ[48]	τῷ κυρίῳ Χριστῷ δουλεύετε·
	3:22c–25a
ποιοῦντες τὸ θέλημα τοῦ θεοῦ,	φοβούμενοι τὸν κύριον. ὃ ἐὰν ποιῆτε,
ἐκ ψυχῆς	ἐκ ψυχῆς ἐργάζεσθε,
7 μετ' εὐνοίας δουλεύοντες, ὡς τῷ κυρίῳ καὶ οὐκ ἀνθρώποις,	ὡς τῷ κυρίῳ καὶ οὐκ ἀνθρώποις,
8 εἰδότες ὅτι ἕκαστος,	εἰδότες ὅτι
ἐάν τι ποιήσῃ ἀγαθόν,	
τοῦτο κομίσεται παρὰ κυρίου,	ἀπὸ κυρίου ἀπολήμψεσθε
	τὴν ἀνταπόδοσιν τῆς κληρονομίας· . . . . ὁ γὰρ ἀδικῶν κομίσεται ὃ ἠδίκησεν,
εἴτε δοῦλος εἴτε ἐλεύθερος.[49]	4:1
9 Καὶ οἱ κύριοι, τὰ αὐτὰ ποιεῖτε πρὸς αὐτούς, ἀνιέντες τὴν ἀπειλήν, εἰδότες ὅτι καὶ αὐτῶν καὶ ὑμῶν ὁ κύριός	Οἱ κύριοι, τὸ δίκαιον καὶ τὴν ἰσότητα τοῖς δούλοις παρέχεσθε, εἰδότες ὅτι καὶ ὑμεῖς ἔχετε κύριον

Other Pauline Parallels

Gal. 1:10b
ἢ ζητῶ ἀνθρώποις ἀρέσκειν;
εἰ ἔτι ἀνθρώποις ἤρεσκον,

Χριστοῦ δοῦλος οὐκ ἂν ἤμην.

Rom. 12:2b
τὸ θέλημα τοῦ θεοῦ

See below

Gal. 6:10b
ἐργαζώμεθα τὸ ἀγαθὸν πρὸς πάντας,

II Cor. 5:10b
ἵνα κομίσηται ἕκαστος τὰ διὰ τοῦ σώματος
πρὸς ἃ ἔπραξεν,

Gal. 3:28b
οὐκ ἔνι δοῦλος οὐδὲ ἐλεύθερος,

εἴτε ἀγαθὸν εἴτε φαῦλον.

---

[48] I Cor. 7:22b, ὁ ἐλεύθερος κληθεὶς δοῦλός ἐστιν Χριστοῦ.
[49] Cf. I Cor. 12:13b, εἴτε δοῦλοι εἴτε ἐλεύθεροι.

EPHESIANS 6	Colossian Parallels
ἐστιν ἐν οὐρανοῖς,	ἐν οὐρανῷ.
	3:25b
καὶ προσωπολημψία οὐκ ἔστιν παρ' αὐτῷ.	καὶ οὐκ ἔστιν προσωπολημψία.
10 Τοῦ λοιποῦ	
	1:11a
ἐνδυναμοῦσθε ἐν κυρίῳ	ἐν πάσῃ δυνάμει δυναμούμενοι
καὶ ἐν τῷ κράτει τῆς ἰσχύος αὐτοῦ.	κατὰ τὸ κράτος τῆς δόξης αὐτοῦ
11 ἐνδύσασθε τὴν πανοπλίαν τοῦ θεοῦ[50]	
πρὸς τὸ δύνασθαι ὑμᾶς στῆναι	
πρὸς τὰς μεθοδίας τοῦ διαβόλου·	
12 ὅτι οὐκ ἔστιν ἡμῖν ἡ πάλη	
	1:16b
πρὸς αἷμα καὶ σάρκα,	τὰ ὁρατὰ καὶ τὰ ἀόρατα,
	εἴτε θρόνοι εἴτε κυριότητες
ἀλλὰ πρὸς τὰς ἀρχάς,	εἴτε ἀρχαὶ
πρὸς τὰς ἐξουσίας,	εἴτε ἐξουσίαι·
πρὸς τοὺς κοσμοκράτορας	

[50] Luke 11:22b, τὴν πανοπλίαν αὐτοῦ αἴρει. Wisd. 5:17a, λήψεται πανοπλίαν τὸν ζῆλον αὐτοῦ.

Other Pauline Parallels

Rom. 2:11
οὐ γάρ ἐστιν προσωπολημψία παρὰ τῷ θεῷ.

Gal. 6:17a
Τοῦ λοιποῦ

Phil. 4:13
πάντα ἰσχύω ἐν τῷ ἐνδυναμοῦντί με.

II Thess. 1:9b
"καὶ ἀπὸ τῆς δόξης τῆς ἰσχύος αὐτοῦ,"

Rom. 13:12b, cf. 14
ἐνδυσώμεθα [δὲ] τὰ ὅπλα τοῦ φωτός.

I Cor. 16:13
Γρηγορεῖτε, στήκετε ἐν τῇ πίστει, ἀνδρίζεσθε, κραταιοῦσθε.

II Cor. 2:11
ἵνα μὴ πλεονεκτηθῶμεν ὑπὸ τοῦ Σατανᾶ, οὐ γὰρ αὐτοῦ τὰ νοήματα ἀγνοοῦμεν.

I Cor. 15:50b; cf. Gal. 1:16
σὰρξ καὶ αἷμα

Rom. 8:38b
οὔτε ἄγγελοι οὔτε ἀρχαὶ . . . .

οὔτε δυνάμεις

Phil. 3:1a
Τὸ λοιπόν,

Rom. 4:20b;
cf. I Cor. 16:13
ἀλλὰ ἐνεδυναμώθη τῇ πίστει,

II Cor. 10:3, 4
Ἐν σαρκὶ γὰρ περιπατοῦντες οὐ κατὰ σάρκα στρατευόμεθα,—

τὰ γὰρ ὅπλα τῆς στρατείας ἡμῶν οὐ σαρκικὰ

ἀλλὰ δυνατὰ τῷ θεῷ πρὸς καθαίρεσιν ὀχυρωμάτων,—
Cf. I Cor. 2:6, 8

EPHESIANS 6	Colossian Parallels
τοῦ σκότους τούτου, πρὸς τὰ πνευματικὰ τῆς πονηρίας ἐν τοῖς ἐπουρανίοις.	
13 διὰ τοῦτο ἀναλάβετε τὴν πανοπλίαν τοῦ θεοῦ,[51]	3:12a Ἐνδύσασθε οὖν
ἵνα δυνηθῆτε ἀντιστῆναι[52] ἐν τῇ ἡμέρᾳ τῇ πονηρᾷ καὶ ἅπαντα κατεργασάμενοι στῆναι.	4:12b ἵνα σταθῆτε τέλειοι καὶ πεπληροφορημένοι ἐν παντὶ θελήματι τοῦ θεοῦ.
14 στῆτε οὖν "περιζωσάμενοι τὴν ὀσφὺν" ὑμῶν "ἐν ἀληθείᾳ,"[53] καὶ "ἐνδυσάμενοι" "τὸν θώρακα τῆς δικαιοσύνης,"[54]	See 4:12b above
15 καὶ ὑποδησάμενοι "τοὺς πόδας" "ἐν ἑτοιμασίᾳ" "τοῦ εὐαγγελίου τῆς εἰρήνης,"[55]	

[51] Luke 11:22b, τὴν πανοπλίαν αὐτοῦ αἴρει. Wisd. 5:17a, λήψεται πανοπλίαν τὸν ζῆλον αὐτοῦ.

[52] Luke 21:15b, ᾗ οὐ δυνήσονται ἀντιστῆναι.

[53] Isa. 11:5, καὶ ἔσται δικαιοσύνῃ ἐζωσμένος τὴν ὀσφὺν αὐτοῦ, καὶ ἀληθείᾳ εἰλημένος τὰς πλευράς.

[54] Isa. 59:17a, καὶ ἐνεδύσατο δικαιοσύνην ὡς θώρακα.

[55] Isa. 52:7b, ὡς πόδες εὐαγγελιζομένου ἀκοὴν εἰρήνης.

OTHER PAULINE PARALLELS

I Thess. 5:5b
Οὐκ ἐσμὲν νυκτὸς οὐδὲ σκότους·

Cf. I Cor. 14:1b
ζηλοῦτε δὲ τὰ πνευματικά,

Cf. I Cor. 15:40; Phil. 2:10

Rom. 13:12b
ἐνδυσώμεθα [δὲ]
τὰ ὅπλα τοῦ φωτός.

I Thess. 5:8b
"ἐνδυσάμενοι"
"θώρακα" πίστεως καὶ ἀγάπης

EPHESIANS 6	Colossian Parallels
	3:12a, 14a
16 ἐν πᾶσιν ἀναλαβόντες	Ἐνδύσασθε οὖν . . . . ἐπὶ πᾶσι δὲ τούτοις
τὸν θυρεὸν τῆς πίστεως,[56] ἐν ᾧ δυνήσεσθε	τὴν ἀγάπην,
πάντα τὰ βέλη τοῦ πονηροῦ [τὰ] πεπυρωμένα σβέσαι·	
17 καὶ "τὴν περικεφαλαίαν" "τοῦ σωτηρίου" δέξασθε,[57] καὶ "τὴν μάχαιραν τοῦ πνεύματος," ὅ ἐστιν "ῥῆμα θεοῦ,"[58]	
	4:2a
18 διὰ πάσης προσευχῆς καὶ δεήσεως,	Τῇ προσευχῇ προσκαρτερεῖτε,
προσευχόμενοι ἐν παντὶ καιρῷ	Cf. vs. 3 below
	1:8b
ἐν πνεύματι,	ἐν πνεύματι.
	4:2b–3a
καὶ εἰς αὐτὸ ἀγρυπνοῦντες ἐν πάσῃ προσκαρτερήσει καὶ δεήσει	γρηγοροῦντες ἐν αὐτῇ ἐν εὐχαριστίᾳ (see above)
	προσευχόμενοι ἅμα καὶ περὶ ἡμῶν,
	1:4b
περὶ πάντων τῶν ἁγίων,	εἰς πάντας τοὺς ἁγίους

[56] Wisd. 5:19, λήψεται ἀσπίδα ἀκαταμάχητον ὁσιότητα.

[57] Isa. 59:17b, καὶ περιέθετο περικεφαλαίαν σωτηρίου ἐπὶ τῆς κεφαλῆς.

[58] Isa. 49:2a, καὶ ἔθηκεν τὸ στόμα μου ὡς μάχαιραν ὀξεῖαν.

Other Pauline Parallels

I Thess. 5:8b
"ἐνδυσάμενοι"

"θώρακα" πίστεως καὶ ἀγάπης

II Thess. 3:3b
καὶ φυλάξει ἀπὸ τοῦ πονηροῦ.

I Thess. 5:8c
καὶ "περικεφαλαίαν"
ἐλπίδα "σωτηρίας·"

Phil. 4:6b
ἐν παντὶ τῇ προσευχῇ καὶ τῇ δεήσει

I Cor. 14:15b
προσεύξομαι

τῷ πνεύματι,

I Thess. 5:17, 18
ἀδιαλείπτως προσεύχεσθε,

ἐν παντὶ εὐχαριστεῖτε·
Rom. 2:29b; 8:9b
ἐν πνεύματι,

Phil. 4:22a
ἀσπάζονται ὑμᾶς πάντες οἱ ἅγιοι,

II Cor. 13:12b
Ἀσπάζονται ὑμᾶς οἱ ἅγιοι πάντες.

EPHESIANS 6	Colossian Parallels
	4:3b, 4
19 καὶ ὑπὲρ ἐμοῦ, ἵνα μοι δοθῇ λόγος	καὶ περὶ ἡμῶν, ἵνα ὁ θεὸς ἀνοίξῃ ἡμῖν θύραν τοῦ λόγου,
ἐν ἀνοίξει τοῦ στόματός μου,	See above
ἐν παρρησίᾳ γνωρίσαι[59]	λαλῆσαι
τὸ μυστήριον [τοῦ εὐαγγελίου][60]	τὸ μυστήριον τοῦ χριστοῦ,
20 ὑπὲρ οὗ πρεσβεύω ἐν ἁλύσει,[61]	δι' ὃ καὶ δέδεμαι,
ἵνα ἐν αὐτῷ παρρησιάσωμαι ὡς δεῖ με λαλῆσαι.	ἵνα φανερώσω αὐτὸ ὡς δεῖ με λαλῆσαι.
	2:1a
21 Ἵνα δὲ εἰδῆτε καὶ ὑμεῖς	Θέλω γὰρ ὑμᾶς εἰδέναι See vs. 8 below
	4:7, 8
τὰ κατ' ἐμέ, τί πράσσω, πάντα γνωρίσει ὑμῖν Τύχικος ὁ ἀγαπητὸς ἀδελφὸς καὶ πιστὸς διάκονος ἐν κυρίῳ,	Τὰ κατ' ἐμέ πάντα γνωρίσει ὑμῖν Τύχικος ὁ ἀγαπητὸς ἀδελφὸς καὶ πιστὸς διάκονος καὶ σύνδουλος ἐν κυρίῳ,
22 ὃν ἔπεμψα πρὸς ὑμᾶς εἰς αὐτὸ τοῦτο ἵνα γνῶτε τὰ περὶ ἡμῶν καὶ παρακαλέσῃ τὰς καρδίας ὑμῶν.	ὃν ἔπεμψα πρὸς ὑμᾶς εἰς αὐτὸ τοῦτο ἵνα γνῶτε τὰ περὶ ἡμῶν καὶ παρακαλέσῃ τὰς καρδίας ὑμῶν,

[61] Acts 28:20b, τὴν ἅλυσιν ταύτην περίκειμαι.

[59] 2:15b, ἐν παρρησίᾳ.
[60] 2:2b τοῦ μυστηρίου τοῦ θεοῦ.

Other Pauline Parallels

Rom. 15:30b, 31a
ὑπὲρ ἐμοῦ πρὸς τὸν θεόν,
ἵνα ῥυσθῶ

II Cor. 6:11a
Τὸ στόμα ἡμῶν ἀνέῳγεν πρὸς ὑμᾶς,

I Cor. 2:1b
καταγγέλλων ὑμῖν

τὸ μυστήριον τοῦ θεοῦ,

II Cor. 5:20a
Ὑπὲρ Χριστοῦ οὖν πρεσβεύομεν

I Thess. 2:2b
ἐπαρρησιασάμεθα ἐν τῷ θεῷ ἡμῶν λαλῆσαι
πρὸς ὑμᾶς τὸ εὐαγγέλιον τοῦ θεοῦ

Philem. 9b
τοιοῦτος ὢν ὡς Παῦλος πρεσβύτης νυνὶ δὲ καὶ δέσμιος Χριστοῦ Ἰησοῦ,—

I Cor. 2:12b
ἵνα εἰδῶμεν

I Cor. 9:17a
εἰ γὰρ ἑκὼν τοῦτο πράσσω,

Philem. 12a
ὃν ἀνέπεμψά σοι αὐτόν,

---

[59] Phil. 1:20b, ἐν πάσῃ παρρησίᾳ.

EPHESIANS 6	Colossian Parallels
23 Εἰρήνη τοῖς ἀδελφοῖς καὶ ἀγάπη μετὰ πίστεως See below ἀπὸ θεοῦ πατρὸς καὶ κυρίου Ἰησοῦ Χριστοῦ.	
24 Ἡ χάρις μετὰ πάντων τῶν ἀγαπώντων τὸν κύριον ἡμῶν Ἰησοῦν Χριστὸν ἐν ἀφθαρσίᾳ.	4:18*b* ἡ χάρις μεθ' ὑμῶν.

Other Pauline Parallels

Gal. 6:16

καὶ ὅσοι τῷ κανόνι τούτῳ στοιχήσουσιν,
"εἰρήνη" ἐπ' αὐτοὺς καὶ ἔλεος,
καὶ "ἐπὶ τὸν Ἰσραὴλ" τοῦ θεοῦ.
See I Cor. 16:24 below

II Thess. 1:2

χάρις ὑμῖν καὶ εἰρήνη
ἀπὸ θεοῦ πατρὸς καὶ κυρίου
Ἰησοῦ Χριστοῦ.
Cf. Rom. 1:7; I Cor. 1:3; II Cor. 1:2; Gal. 1:3

I Cor. 16:22–24

εἴ τις οὐ φιλεῖ τὸν κύριον, ἤτω ἀνάθεμα. . . .
ἡ χάρις τοῦ κυρίου Ἰησοῦ μεθ' ὑμῶν
ἡ ἀγάπη μου μετὰ πάντων ὑμῶν ἐν Χριστῷ Ἰησοῦ.

I Cor. 15:42b

ἐγείρεται ἐν ἀφθαρσίᾳ·

TABLE OF PASSAGES QUOTED

Gen. 2:24	150		2:11	157
Exod. 20:12	152		2:17, 18	145
Deut. 33:4	90		2:19	143
Ps. 4:5	134		2:21	135
8:7	94		2:28	103
40:7	138		2:29	161
68:19	124		3:22	93
96:7	118		3:23	97
110:1	92		3:24	99, 101, 123
Prov. 2:2	152		3:25	87
23:31	144		3:25, 26	85
Isa. 11:5	158		3:27	101
49:2	160		3:28	101
49:8	136		3:30	125
50:5	152		4:2	101
52:7	106, 158		4:13, 14	113
57:19	105, 106		4:16, 17	113
59:17	158, 160		4:20	157
63:10	136		5:1, 2	105, 117
Jer. 23:24	94		5:2	91, 107
Ezek. 20:41	138		5:8	99
Mic. 5:5	104		5:9	85
Zech. 8:16	134		5:15	85, 101, 115, 125
Wisd. 5:17	156, 158		6:4	91, 133
5:19	160		6:6	133
Mark 3:28	110		6:11	95
Luke 1:75	132		6:12	133
4:1	146		6:16	153
11:22	156, 158		7:22	119
15:13	146		8:7	97
21:15	158		8:9	109, 119, 161
Acts 3:25	118		8:15	83
7:55	146		8:16, 17	89
13:1	108		8:17	113
13:10	134		8:20	131
15:6	108		8:23	89, 137
20:28	126		8:24	101
21:8	126		8:28	87, 117
28:20	162		8:28–30	87
Rev. 13:8	82		8:29	83, 101
17:8	82		8:34	93
Rom. 1:8	89		8:35	121
1:10	89		8:38	95, 121, 157
1:11	83		9:1	133
1:16	89		9:4	103
1:18	141		9:5	125
1:21	91, 131		9:11	87
1:24	97, 133		9:19	87
1:28	91, 141		9:23	91, 99, 119
2:4	85, 99		9:23, 24	87
2:10	135		9:32	101

10:3	131	4:9	103
10:6, 7	127	4:12	135
10:9	149	4:14	139, 153
10:14	89	4:16	139
11:13	109	5:2	137
11:25	131, 151	5:9	111
11:32, 33	99, 115	5:11	139
11:33	85	6:4	123
11:36	95, 117, 123, 125	6:9, 10	141
12:1	123	6:11	149
12:2	97, 133, 143, 145, 155	6:14	93
12:3	115	6:15	151
12:4, 5	125	6:16	151
12:5	95, 113, 135, 151	7:2	151
12:6	125	7:3, 4	149
12:6–8	127	7:17	123
12:10	147	7:20	125
12:13	137	7:22	155
12:19	135	8:2	121
13:3	101	8:5	103, 119
13:9	87, 151	8:6	125
13:12	133, 135, 157, 159	9:17	111, 163
13:12, 13	143	9:24	121
13:13	145	10:11	87
13:14	97, 133	10:17	125
14:11	117	11:1	139
14:15	139	11:3	129, 147, 151
15:13	119	11:11	151
15:19	119	12:2	103
15:20	119	12:6	87
15:30, 31	163	12:13	107, 125, 155
15:31	97	12:27	95, 127
16:19	145	12:28	109, 113, 127
16:25	91, 121	13:2	121
16:25, 26	85, 111, 115	13:8	121
16:26	113	14:1	159
16:27	123	14:12	131
I Cor. 1:4	111	14:15	147, 161
1:6	83	14:16	113
1:27	83	14:20	129
1:29, 30	101	14:24	143
2:1	163	14:26	127, 137
2:6	95, 129	15:9	115
2:7	83, 85, 115, 117	15:24	93
2:7, 8	111	15:27	95
2:8	91	15:28	95
2:10	91, 111	15:34	135
2:12	97, 163	15:42	165
3:1	167	15:50	157
3:6, 7	109	15:51	151
3:9	109	16:13	119, 157
3:10	109, 145	16:22–24	165
3:11	109	II Cor. 1:1	121
3:12	109	1:1–3	83
3:16	109, 119	1:3	91
3:16, 17	109	1:12	97
4:5	143	1:22	89, 119, 137

TABLE OF PASSAGES QUOTED

2:11	135, 157		5:2	109
3:4	117		5:3	131
3:12	117		5:4	103
4:1	117		5:13	147
4:4	91		5:19–21	141
4:16	117, 119		5:22, 23	143
5:10	155		6:10	107, 135, 155
5:17	101, 107		6:16	103, 165
5:19	85		6:17	157
5:20	163		Phil. 1:3, 4	147
6:2	137		1:9	91
6:7	89		1:11	85, 87, 89
6:11	163		1:13	123
6:14	143		1:20	163
6:16	109		1:27	107
7:15	153		2:2	123
8:18	117		2:3	123, 147
9:8	101		2:9, 10	93
9:14	93, 121		2:12	153
9:14, 15	85		2:13	85, 87
10:1	109, 123		3:1	157
10:3, 4	157		3:3	103
11:2	149		3:10	93
11:3	133		3:11	127
11:6	111		3:20	107, 147
11:10	133		3:21	93, 131
11:31	91		4:6	161
12:2	127		4:13	157
12:11	145		4:18	139, 143
12:19	127		4:22	161
12:21	133, 139		Col. 1:1, 2	82
13:4	93		1:3	90
13:5	119		1:4	82, 88, 160
13:9	127		1:5	88
13:12	161		1:8	112, 160
Gal. 1:4	87, 145		1:9	82, 84, 88, 90, 110, 120
1:5	123		1:10	100, 122, 128
1:10	150		1:11	92, 118, 156
1:12	111		1:12	86, 88, 90
1:13	111, 133		1:13	96
1:15, 16	115		1:13, 14	84
2:7	115		1:14	88
2:15	97		1:16	92, 116, 118, 156
2:20	129, 139, 149		1:18	94, 128, 146
3:2	89		1:19	94, 118
3:3	145		1:19, 20	126
3:5	121		1:20	84, 86, 104, 106
3:14	83, 89		1:21	96, 100, 102, 104, 130
3:26	83		1:22	82, 104, 106, 148
3:26–29	113		1:23	114, 118
3:27	133		1:24	108, 116
3:28	105, 155		1:25	86, 110, 114
4:4	87		1:25, 26	114
4:5	83		1:26	84, 110, 122
4:8, 9	103		1:26, 27	90
4:16	129		1:27	114, 118
4:28	97		1:28	128

1:29	114, 120, 130	4:2, 3	160
2:1	116, 162	4:3	110
2:2	162	4:3, 4	162
2:2, 3	120	4:5	144
2:4	130, 140	4:6	136
2:6, 7	132	4:7, 8	162
2:7	108, 118, 140	4:12	144, 158
2:8, 9, 10	128	4:16	110
2:9	120	4:18	102, 164
2:10	92	I Thess. 1:2	165
2:11	102	2:2	163
2:12	98	2:7	151
2:13	94, 98	2:12	123
2:14	104	2:13	97
2:15	162	2:20	117
2:18	132	3:10	121
2:19	108, 128, 130	4:5	103
3:1	92, 98	4:8	137
3:3	98, 116	4:9	123
3:5	132, 138	4:11, 12	135
3:5, 6	140	4:13	97, 103
3:6	96	5:5	143, 159
3:7	94, 96	5:7	145
3:8	136, 138, 142	5:8	159, 161
3:8, 9	132, 134	5:9	89, 97
3:10	106, 132	5:17, 18	161
3:11	106	5:18	141, 147
3:12	82, 158	5:19	137
3:12, 13	138	II Thess. 1:9	157
3:12, 14	160	1:11	123
3:12–15	122	2:3, 4	97
3:15	140	2:7	97
3:16	136	2:9	131
3:16–18	146	2:13	83
3:17	140	2:14	113
3:18	150	2:16	99
3:19	148	2:17	137
3:20	142	3:3	161
3:20–23	152	Philem. 1	109, 123
3:22	154	4	91
3:24	154	5	89
3:25	154, 156	6	129
4:1	154	9	123, 163
4:2	160	12	163

www.ingramcontent.com/pod-product-compliance
Lightning Source LLC
Chambersburg PA
CBHW070943160426
43193CB00011B/1789